ADVERTISING *FOR* *PEOPLE* *WHO* *DON'T* *LIKE* ADVERTISING.

BY KESSELSKRAMER

TABLE OF CONTENTS

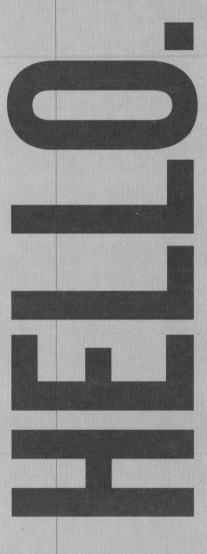

HELLO.

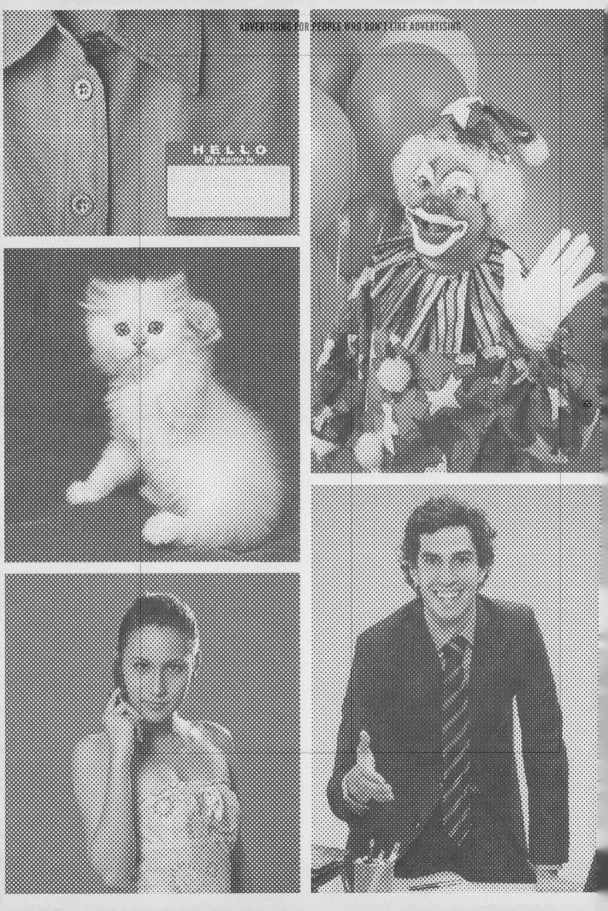

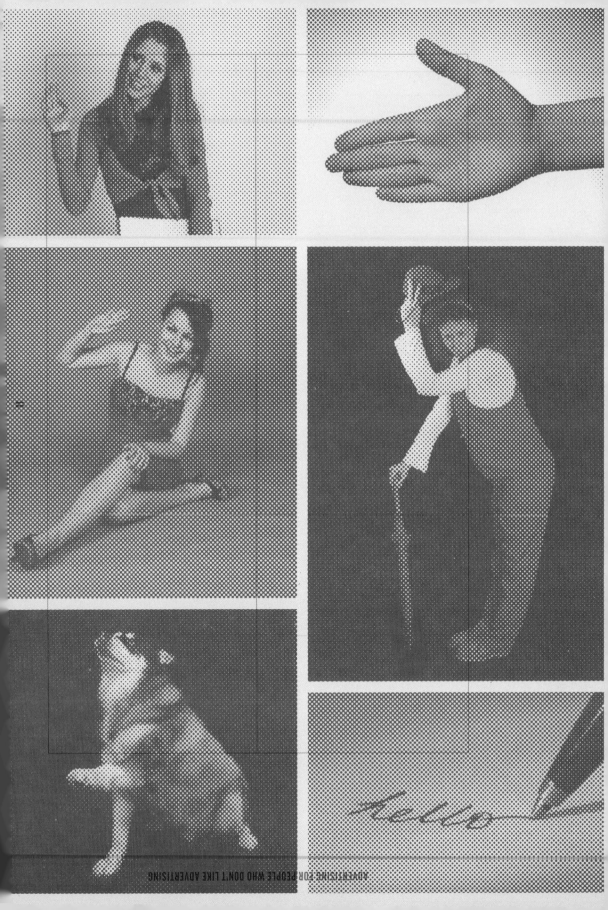

This book is for anyone who's ever been irritated by a commercial break or frustrated by a web banner. In other words, most people.

It was initiated by a company called KesselsKramer, and we know how you feel. We really do.

However, it's only fair to inform you: we make ads. Lots of them.

Amongst many, many other projects, we've worked with global brands to make fashion collections, turned dogshit into mini billboards _fig. 01_ and promoted a Dutch province by staging a mass wedding.

KesselsKramer (KK) began in 1996, born in part from a dislike of adverts in general, as well as the industry conventions that produced them.

One of those conventions was the use of the word "advertising" itself. KK felt that "advertising" stood for a narrow mindset: the assembly-line production of formulaic billboards, TV ads and radio spots.

Instead, KesselsKramer became preoccupied with making "communications." For KK "communications" stood for truthful, human messages that told a brand's story in any and all available media.

Though now common, this approach was then novel: using music videos, books, exhibitions and stunts to support a product was rare to the point of being virtually non-existent.

This love of diversity also under-scored a restlessness that extended beyond advertising. Outside commercial briefs, KesselsKramer spent (and spends) its time expressing creative ideas wherever the possibility arises. After all, an idea is still an idea, whether it comes attached to a sales message or not.

Over time, this version of "communi-cations" came to encompass the publication of books on photography (through KK's in-house publisher) and an own brand, "do," whose

many products aim to make consumer-ism less passive. fig. 01

More accurately, then, this book should be entitled *Communications For People Who Don't Like Advertising* but that wouldn't make much sense to anyone outside KesselsKramer. So it isn't. Instead, we chose *Advertising For People Who Don't Like Advertising*, not just for the sake of clarity but as an invitation to all those who would mess with creative commerce.

This book is motivated by a wish to look outward, to make contact with those we admire, those who question our industry. We wanted to discover what insights they've gained over the last decade or so, a period in which the business was redefined, and re-redefined, and re-re-redefined.

Our collaborators include Alex Bogusky, who left one of the most prestigious creative posts in advertising to work on the biggest of projects: how to help capitalism grow up.

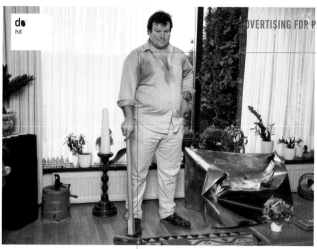

do
hit

NOW EVEN MORE
OF THIS AT
OUR MAIN
ENTRANCE

do
break

Fig. 01: Anti-clockwise from top right: KK's stunt for the Hans Brinker Budget Hotel, possibly the most widely reported dog turd in history. A selection of items from KK's inhouse brand "do," which seeks to make consumerism less passive by asking users to modify its products. Two images from an international fashion collection developed for Absolut.

Renowned designer Stefan Sagmeister explains how quitting work makes you better at working.

The legendary Steve Henry tells how he changed the business of advertising once, and suggests how he would do so again.

Photographer, curator, journalist and all-round Renaissance Man Hans Aarsman ponders the always murky line between advertising and news.

Anthony Burrill visualizes his concerns with communications through design and illustration.

Finally, former music video director, copywriter superstar and educator Mark Fenske tells us what it takes to become a great creative.

But this book isn't a blueprint for a brighter tomorrow. You're not holding a political manifesto, only with pictures. And don't expect footnotes with quotes from peer-reviewed papers. Academically speaking, nothing here would make it on Wikipedia.

Do expect a collage. As well as our contributors' pieces, tales of Kessels-Kramer's own exploits and creative advice, we have examples of contemporary advertising that don't look, feel or think like advertising. These are included to inspire and amuse both you and us.

Before we begin, let's end on a final caveat: along the way, we'll raise more questions than we answer. And most of what you'll read is pure, subjective, unverifiable opinion. Opinion formed over long years, long hours, some success and more failure… but opinion nonetheless.

One of those opinions has to do with a drift we see within the industry, a movement toward a more positive form of advertising. So select a seating position of your choice, open a refreshing beverage and we'll attempt some cultural commentary.

FAIRY TALES FOR

TREND SPOT-TERS.

Here's a story about Western society.

It goes like this:

Sometime in the last twenty years, we all turned into hippies. Some of us became big hippies, some medium-sized hippies, and some quite small hippies — hippies in suits with BMWs. Nevertheless, compared to "Homus Eighties," we all might as well be playing acoustic guitars with sunflowers in our unwashed hair.

As part of this general hippification, products and services that promote a more selfless consumerism became the norm.

Take recycling, for instance. Once exclusively for New Agers, but now widespread and unremarkable, with even the most conservative householder separating glass from plastics, and paper from organic compost.

Or take biological food. Our indifference to what we eat is waning. Slowly we're voting with our store cards, slowly produce is becoming friendly: to people, chickens, pigs,

fish, olives, tomatoes. Even the peanuts in peanut butter die with grace and dignity. And words like "by-catch" and "bio-industry" can be used in daily speech without anyone requesting a dictionary definition.

Today, sustainability is a topic for Presidential speeches.

Today, nobody thinks it's a grand statement if you buy Fair Trade. Today, multinationals spend millions on commercials touting their environmental good deeds.

Today, Oscar winners include *Inside Job*, a complex, partisan documentary about banking corruption and the wrong inflicted by money.

Even if we're not exactly a species of Joni Mitchells just yet, the West seems on course for Planet Hippy.

At some point, these attitudes found their way down to what's traditionally seen as a moral basement: advertising (one floor down from lawyers,

take a right at the guys who train child soldiers).

About as socially acceptable as arms dealing, advertising is still considered "poison gas" (to quote the legendary art director George Lois). At the time of writing, Morgan Spurlock has released a new film about the perniciousness of branded content, and the likes of Peter Joseph's Zeitgeist Movement condemns commercial creativity as the devil's work. Mostly, ads are judged to be subtle manipulation, emotional blackmail or simply plain old remorseless propaganda.

We're not disagreeing.

But while these opinions are mostly/ all true, there's a counter-culture even within the ad industry. In the nineties, agencies began to emerge that swept the *Mad Men* stereotype aside, embodying a different set of values, perhaps closer to the present's more responsible outlook.

These agencies were reformers on all levels. They experimented with more liberal, open-minded creative practices, more transparent business policies and more grown-up ethics. They turned down tobacco, they turned down airlines, they turned down reactionary political parties. A massively influential example of this type of agency is Howell Henry Chaldecott Lury, the co-founder of which, Steve Henry, appears in these pages.

These agencies could do what they did because advertising is basically morally neutral. Believe it or not, advertising's nature doesn't inherently make you anxious, or create a burning desire for pointless junk. Granted, that's how it's most often used, but that isn't what it *is*.

One of the contributors to this book, Alex Bogusky, defines advertising as "asking for attention," and likens its ethics to sex: you can do some pretty horrible things involving sex, and you can do some pretty amazing ones

too (make a family, for instance). Ultimately, sex and advertising are just sex and advertising. Both are only as warped as the people involved.

In short, when the values of the people making ads change, so does the great snotty beast itself. To be fair, this change feels glacial, but it's a pretty fast-moving glacier, one with plenty of cracks, one that occasionally, very occasionally, doesn't feel like a glacier at all, but a slow and slushy river.

One of the primary reasons for change is that, ultimately, advertising is a creative industry, and creativity is all about transformation.

Now, from the outside, all those endless standardized ads for face wash and tampons don't look remotely creative, but the process that spews them out is a creative one, absolutely, positively, definitely. Trust us on this.

Behind every horrific model skating along a beach at sunset, there are a hundred, a thousand, wonderful ideas. In fact, there's a graveyard full of them, each one murdered by fear, compromise and office politics. But to say that these wonderful creative ideas died isn't the same as saying they never lived. And it sure isn't the same as saying there aren't a hundred thousand more where they came from.

So let's think glass almost half-full.

Probability states that the new responsible societal attitudes described above will increasingly manifest themselves in advertising (which very often only reflects what the world is thinking). There will come a day when that dark army of skating models is struck down and replaced, one by one, by fantastic ideas. Perhaps ideas that provoke and engage, instead of comparing you negatively to some tedious Photoshopped rollerblading bint. Or perhaps ideas that just make you giggle, or feel better disposed toward whatever's happening in your day.

The point is: you can't be in a creative business like advertising without being experimental, and you can't be experimental without questioning the status quo — even if the status quo is usually paying your bills.

Question hard enough and long enough, and good things will happen.

From inside advertising you can see glimmers of this, and not just from agencies.

As of a few years ago, even the largest, staunchest corporations have put "responsibility" at the heart of their internal conversations. It's also standard practice for clients to request not simplistic old-school ads, but multi-disciplinary projects encouraging creative collaboration with their product's audience. Open source over hard sell.

So this book promotes a type of advertising that we can all live with: brand stories that are honest, engaging and open. It's a style that's been around for a while, but is only now evolving in a way that's consistent and long-term.

Or so we hope.

Like we said, this is a story, and stories are often merely wishful thinking.

WHY NOW

(PART 2).

It's beyond a cliché to state what we're about to state but let's state it anyway — for the sake of clarity, if not insight.

Here goes. The Internet is an enormous, magical, terrifying, brilliant, endless miracle that has changed all our lives beyond recognition. It has revolutionized, and continues to revolutionize, all aspects of business.

It does so in time-spans that are ruthlessly short.

The "new industries" of a decade ago are now about as relevant as a weaving loom in a pre-Industrial Revolution crofter's cottage. When was the last time you went into a DVD rental store? And if your answer is "recently" then why? (Besides asking for directions to the Mac shop.)

But while our upheavals may be fast, technology-driven and merciless, that's where the easy Industrial Revolution comparisons end.

Whereas the Victorians subjected everyone and his four-year-old child to bone-breaking factory labour, online has made business and communications egalitarian. Suddenly, everyone is a writer — even if all they're writing is an email. Suddenly, everyone is a designer — even if all they're designing is a Christmas card with a web-based Adobe tutorial. Suddenly, everyone can develop their business idea of a lifetime by tweeting about it, testing potential names with Google adwords, and even hiring staff via Amazon's Mechanical Turk.

The Internet and associated technologies have ripped apart and rebuilt not just the creative side of business, but the means of distributing the products you create. Just outsource a website build to the Far East, hook that site up to PayPal and design an email signature — minimum overheads, almost minimum risk.

And whereas the language of nineteenth-century industrial capitalism sounds exhausting and confrontational ("competition," "demand," "profit"), the language of Internet business is about as aggressive as Sunday morning cartoons: "giving," "sharing," "gifts."

But while it's cuddly, it works.

Marketing author Seth Godin most famously gave away his book *Purple Cow* for free over the web, and still managed to make it a success. A substantial one. As of 2011 he's engaged in turning his experiment into an honest-to-God stable platform for distributing books, some by well-known writers, all of them gratis.

Cartoonist Hugh MacLeod sends free daily cartoons to subscribers. His thinking is that, given time, these cartoons will find their way to people who'll pay good money for original pieces. His work has resulted in a *Wall Street Journal* bestselling book, so perhaps he has a point.

Chances are you know some or all of these approaches — unless you're a member of an undiscovered tribe in the remote Amazon. Even then: you probably get *Digital Buzz* on your iPad.

What you might not know is how this most familiar of revolutions has influenced advertising's mainstream. Because the Internet is social and democratic, the brands using it effectively are required to become equally accessible. This means more than simply asking people to click "like" on Facebook. It means real engagement, an involvement that you can't force but must be chosen — bullying people into loving your monolithic corporation via an online community doesn't work.

Increasingly, this leads to companies expressing themselves in a tone that's less strident and less one-sided. No longer do brands talk at you, preaching like the least socially skilled guest at a party. Sometimes they talk *with* you, asking how you're doing, how your soulmate's doing, listening to your views, respecting your opinion, even requesting advice. Occasionally they're as sincere as a contestant on *America's Next Top Model*, but at least they try.

Naturally, social brands talking via an inherently social medium has an effect on agencies.

Below is how the above came to be.

Or rather: our version of it.

A BRIEF HISTORY OF

SELLING STUFF

(ACCORDING TO KESSELSKRAMER).

There are several paradigm shifts in the history of advertising.

One was the moment when the first Egyptian turned papyrus into a poster. Another was the creative revolution of the sixties, when advertising creatives first began working in teams.

And another took place roughly last Wednesday.

Until very, very recently, most of advertising was divided by media specialties. If you wanted a multi-million-dollar cinema commercial, you went to one type of agency. If you wanted a mass letter informing housewives about an exciting development in frozen foods, you went to another.

In turn, the men and women who created ads defined themselves by whatever media they focused on.

ATL meant "Above the Line" and represented where most people wanted to be: making TV commercials,

hanging out with photographers shooting press ads on beaches, driving past enormous billboards of their work at the weekends.

ATL was renowned for a certain type of, um, confidence.

After all, sitting around a film set being handed mocha-choca-lattes or seeing your ideas replicated twenty-feet tall is a huge ego kick… and can fairly easily lead to the mistaken belief that you're in The Rolling Stones (which is odd, because "washing powder salesperson" is a more accurate job description).

And then there was BTL, or "Below the Line." Rather unfairly, BTL was seen as ATL's awkward, trailer-dwelling, snaggle-toothed cousin. Mostly by people who worked in ATL.

BTL dealt with the less glamorous end of the business. Direct mail was produced, vouchers designed and wobblers created. (A "wobbler" is a plastic strip attached to a supermarket shelf. You don't need to hang out on a beach with a photographer in order to create a wobbler).

While BTL wasn't quite as showbiz, darling, it was more effective. Perhaps not always creatively, but from a purely business perspective your shilling was better invested in a well-crafted pamphlet. Daring, expensive TV ads are career Russian roulette: clients lose their jobs if the mild uptake they were expecting turns into a nosedive of complaints and negative PR. By contrast, a brochure is always a bargain, and its success is directly measured by the number of responses you get to the voucher printed in the back.

One way to understand the ATL/BTL divisions is "sex" and "work." ATL was "sex." At its best, it was the craft of creating desire. In its most extreme manifestation you bought into a belief system, not just a product. The ultimate example of

this is Nike, still referenced to death in every meeting every day within the advertising industry. You bought Nike and you stood for optimism, struggle and victory (echoed in the name itself, of course).

And that was at the very least. At most, buying Nike meant joining a modern religion, something that gave your life purpose and meaning (as argued by James Twitchell in *Adcult USA*). BTL, meanwhile, was about getting on with it and paying the bills. There is little religion-making involved in sticking a "2 for 1" on dog food down your local supermarket.

Now, these definitions are somewhat artificial. There are plenty of examples of brilliant experimentation within BTL. And there are plenty of hard-headed sales ads on your TV every night. But there is a general truth in the "sex" and "work" descriptions, and perhaps also a general prejudice. Generally speaking, it was a lot harder to make outstanding

work in BTL, and (generally speaking) a lot more fun to enter the paradise of ATL. The two never crossed paths. ATL and BTL folk were rarely even seen in the same building together. When they joined forces true collaboration was limited, submerged in hierarchy. The ATL agency passed its ideas down to the BTL office for adaptation into… whatever it is they did. Leaflets or something.

These divisions applied for years. In fact, you might argue that they apply still, in old-fashioned agencies run mostly by greying Twitter virgins. However, for the most part, a time of change eventually swept across the kingdom. It came in the form of things that looked like TVs, only with things that looked like typewriters attached to the bottom.

Its name was Digital.

At first, online advertising was dispatched to the BTL ghetto. The product of early digital agencies was seen as a sort of futuristic

ITS NAME WAS DIGITAL.

direct marketing, wobblers for the web, animated brochures. Predictably, the people seeing things this way were ATL agencies, and they were doing their best to preserve a way of life involving as many palm trees and helicopter shots as possible. To be honest: who could blame them?

Unfortunately for ATL, Digital proved to be a growth market. More than a growth market, it was a fecund jungle of creative and technological innovation.

Whereas advertising journals once wrote sceptical articles doubting Digital in every edition, soon they started giving special awards to Digital agencies. Moments after that, even the idea of Digital awards became strange and quaint. Why? Because Digital as a category was ceasing to exist. It was so successful that it became irrelevant, it became everything. Where Digital stopped and other forms of advertising began now seemed problematic: press ads existed only to encourage visits to

websites, thirty-second television ads premiered on YouTube.

The very notion of talking to the public through one medium seemed bizarre. Suddenly, making a one-off, big-budget TV commercial felt like advertising time travel, back through a mysteriously glowing portal marked "1980s."

Finally, there was an irony of the delicious variety. Some years ago the more open-minded, bigger ATL agencies abruptly decided they were no longer ATL. To some degree, they had said this for ages, but for the most part little was done beyond producing Power-Point presentations and spin.

Now, however, ATL meant it.

Whole Digital departments sprung up over night, stuffed into the designer attics of international ATL agencies. Being a creative meant replacing your battered leather portfolio with an online one, full of online examples

of online work. Job interviews in the most traditional agencies opened with "The future is online. What's your online experience?" Frequently, a director's most interesting work had never appeared on TV, but on a website.

Which brings us to the present: an industry that's as unsure as it's possible to be. There are ATL agencies that still farm their work out to Digital agencies. There are ATL agencies that no longer call themselves ATL. There are BTL agencies that have become Digital. There are Digital agencies that have as much power as a traditional ATL ever did. There are Digital agencies that merely program, and Digital agencies that supply creative. There are BTL agencies that make TV and radio ads. There are ATL agencies that could make a hundred glitzy cinema ads a year, but would rather make websites.

Every possible variation of every possible model is being explored, often within the same company. It's an exciting, messy time.

It's a time when advertising can be hated in whole new ways, but also occasionally admired for its bravery and experimentation.

All in all, the industry as a whole feels like a frontier again — a bit rough, but as different from the days of *Nine Out Of Ten Doctors Smoke Camels* as an abacus to a trumpet-playing robot.

Welcome to advertising's Wild West, where the cowboys wear limited-edition Converse and go on detox weeks to Thailand.

KESSELS-KRAMER

(A GUIDE FOR THOSE WHO'VE NEVER HEARD OF US).

Advertising For People Who Don't Like Advertising was initiated by a group of creative people working from a church in Amsterdam.

The church features original stained-glass windows, an exquisite marble altar and (for reasons best left unexplained) a gigantic wooden fortress where the pews should be. Once the chapel for a local order of nuns, it is now the home of a communications agency called Kessels-Kramer. *fig. 02*

KK was founded by an art director/ copywriter team, after they'd been fired from a prestigious London agency. Frustrated by the politics, slow production schedules and routine of large agency life, Johan Kramer and Erik Kessels aimed to create a less structured, more prolific type of company, one centred on finding new means of expression for communications.

From the start, Kramer and Kessels fiddled with advertising's institutions. This fiddling included interesting

business choices, as well as the frequent following of slightly anarchic whims.

Among the whims:

THE GREAT COFFEE MACHINE VENDETTA.

Coffee machines were banned for the first years of the company's existence. Also printers. This was because coffee machines and printers were felt to represent corporate advertising at its most banal. Any coffee machine seen within a hundred yards of KesselsKramer was hunted down with brutal efficiency, battered until it gushed espresso over the cobblestones, bundled into a sack and tossed in the nearest canal. After many, many years the persecution of innocent coffee machines was relaxed due to one fundamental need: humans like coffee. Today, KesselsKramer staff enjoy the fruits of a (slightly nervous) coffee machine on a daily basis.

Among the interesting business choices:

DEATH TO ACCOUNT HANDLERS.

An "account handler" is a cornerstone in the structure of classic agencies. Account handlers are a buffer between agency and client. Traditionally, they present ideas to clients and relay client feedback back to creatives.

There are several reasons for this, but the most common is one you won't find on any agency website.

It is:
Account handlers view most creatives as being too uncivilized to engage in client conversations. A bit too scruffy. A bit too mono-syllabic. Frequently, they are right.

Fig. 02: KesselsKramer's offices look like this. In case you were wondering.

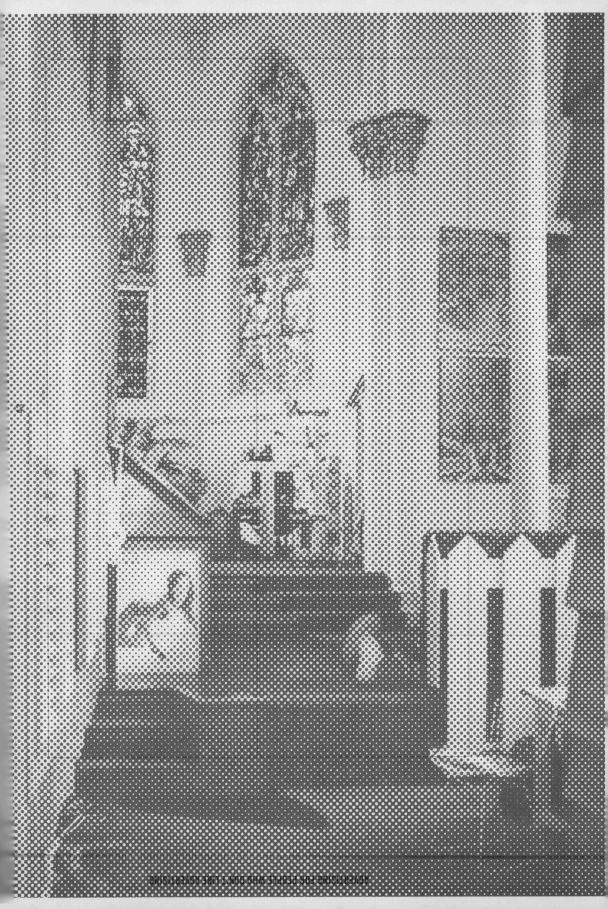

(In turn, most creatives view account handlers as clients-in-disguise. Frequently, they are also right.)

There are two species of account handler.

In some "creatively led" agencies the account handler is demoted to the cruel status of "bag carrier." She/he is the girl/boy who takes presentations to meetings, plugs in the projector, sits in a corner, takes notes, unplugs the projector and carries the presentations back to the agency. They hold doors and make tea. They are geishas in suits.

Of course, you only put people down because they scare the shit out of you.

This leads us to the second type of Accountus Handelitus.

In many agencies account handlers shine. More than shine, they effectively run the place. They are smarter, quicker and infinitely

more professional than creatives. They are also genuinely interested in responding to a client's needs and solving business problems (as opposed to creatives, who are mostly only genuinely interested in winning awards).

These account handlers were frighteningly brilliant at university, and frighteningly brilliant at work. If they ever tried it, they'd probably also be frighteningly brilliant at water polo. They're that kind of person.

Whichever kind of accounts person you were familiar with, to do away with the account handler function entirely was a major departure from accepted agency structure.

KesselsKramer's issue with account handlers wasn't that they were bad people, or scary ones, or ruthless Type A personalities. In fact, many people at KesselsKramer used to be account handlers.

It was simply that the role of account handler can be split over other departments. This hanging, drawing and quartering of the account handler expresses a certain logic, once you strip the job down to its core.

At heart, the account handler's profession can be summarized as talking (with a bunch of emailing on the side). Sometimes this talking is incredibly eloquent and insightful, but it's still mainly about opening your mouth, your neurons doing stuff and words coming out.

KesselsKramer noticed that other people can talk too.

Producers can talk to clients. Strategists can talk to clients. Even creatives can talk to clients, and they're famous for not talking.

You just have to find the right people, train them, believe in them, accept their decisions and forgive

their mistakes. (Actually, encourage their mistakes; mistakes are beautiful and constructive tools.)

Help them discover their inner account handler.

DEATH TO A BUNCH

OF OTHER PEOPLE.

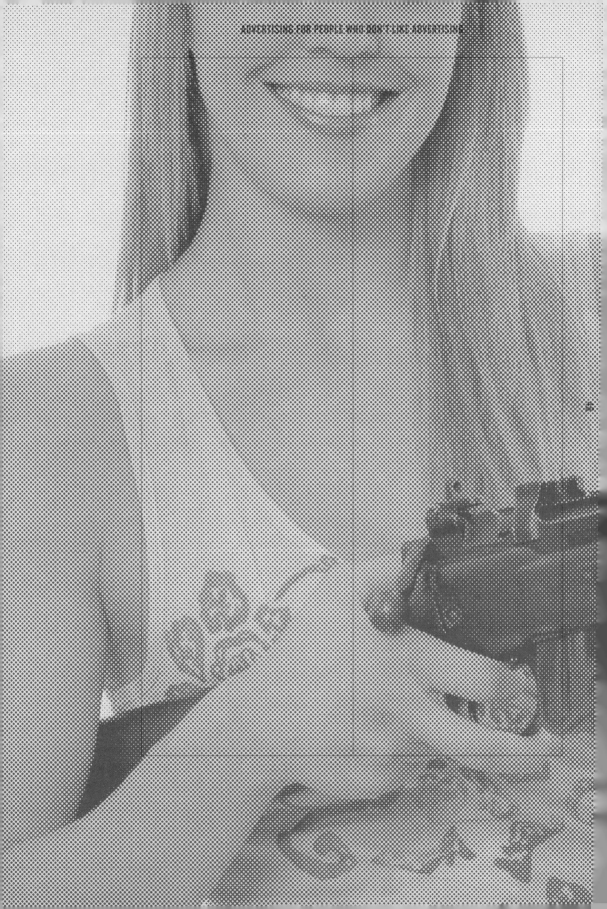

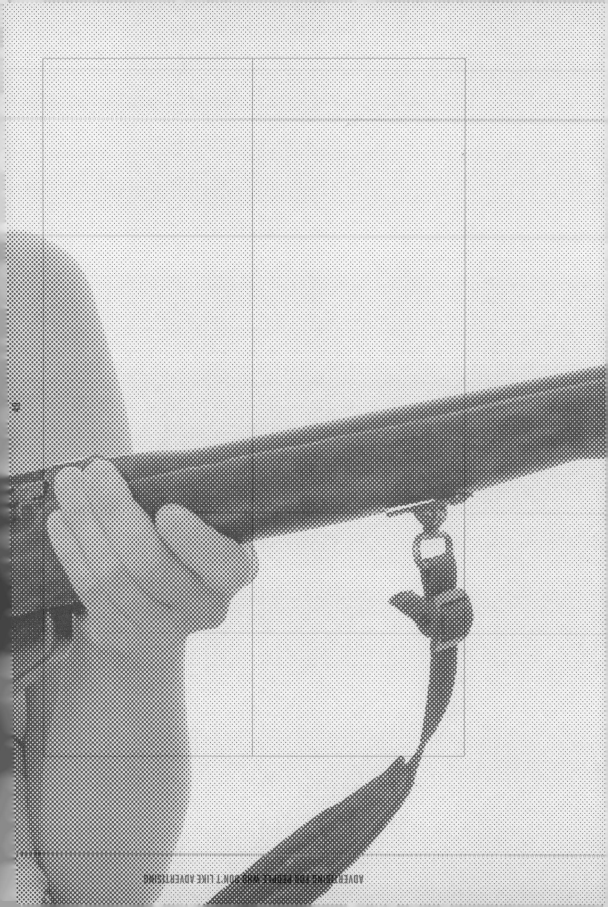

The KesselsKramer company version of a nip/tuck extended to other functions within the traditional agency set-up.

More bits of fat for the plastic surgeon's suction pump included:

TRAFFIC.

Large agencies require someone to manage workflow — assigning briefs to particular teams, as well as overseeing the progress of those teams.

KesselsKramer has a staff of roughly thirty-five people, so the notion of a Traffic Department seemed a little grand.

In fact, it could easily be replaced by the Walking Up To Someone And Asking Them What They're Doing Department. Anyone could join this department, as it required only the ability to saunter over to your colleagues and update them on whatever needed updating.

ART BUYERS.

An art buyer's function hovers somewhere between art director and producer.

Art buyers know the latest illustrators, photographers, models, finger painters – whichever outside parties are required to take a concept through to a fully realized campaign. They book said parties and recommend said parties to creatives.

Again, KesselsKramer's scale meant that art buyers were less than essential. Instead, KesselsKramer creatives are asked to look for their own inspiring collaborators, sometimes also booking and

managing their chosen photographer/illustrator/origami expert. The money side of this usually falls into a producer's remit.

In essence, these alterations boil down to making the making of advertising better by making it less.

You might also say that this is obvious: cut overheads and make life easier. So what?

Well, yes, good point: so what indeed.

But however many times these ideas are raised, agencies, like most companies, remain full of not-very-inspired folk doing semi-useful semi-jobs.

So while there's a degree of plain, smack-you-between-the-eyes common sense to all this, it's also an attitude that's worth repeating and worth discussing.

THE TRIUMPH OF

SMALL.

At several points in its decade and a half, KesselsKramer has had opportunities to grow, sometimes a lot. But even after it eventually expanded to London, both this offshoot and the original Amsterdam office remained compact. This is because we've followed a "Small for the Sake of Small" philosophy.

Why would you turn your back on swimming pools full of money, shiny offices and interns whose sole function is doing your dry-cleaning?

Depends on what your priorities are. A KesselsKramer priority is the flexibility to experiment. Without wishing to sound naïve and deny the importance of putting bread on tables, creativity is more important than profit.

In fact, our view is that creativity is what puts bread on tables. Short term, the quest for large, conservative, wealthy clients will indeed pay the instalments on your sports car. Long term, it'll kill you.

At some point there comes the
realization that you haven't made
anything for years, and what you
have made isn't worth talking about.
Nobody will want to work with
you, because nothing you make
is interesting.

In effect, you've stopped being
a creative advertising agency
and become the producers of
visual wallpaper.

KesselsKramer would rather
stay independent and creative.
Even if that means doing our
own dry-cleaning.

SMALL IS HUMAN.

Not everything you've heard about advertising is true.

Most advertising people are very, very nice and very, very brilliant. Really.

But.

Advertising is indeed a ruthless business.

This isn't due to the people in it, but due to the nature of advertising itself, in which each agency is

(an oft-quoted) "three phone calls away from bankruptcy."

What this means is that three clients leaving a company in quick succession can mean the demise of that company.

As a whole, the industry has been in a state of contraction for decades. Every year is the hardest year to get a job in advertising ever. The business shrinks at the mere mention of a recession, an act of terrorism

or a new device that finally frees people from adverts (TiVo, for example). In fact, "The End of Advertising" is spoken about so often that it becomes a familiar drone for anyone keeping up with the industry press.

Mostly, though, these articles aren't really talking about the end of anything. More often, they actually mean the evolution of the business, perhaps into something unrecogniz-able, perhaps only into some-thing involving more and more and more online.

In other words, talk of a shrinking business is a little misleading. The business isn't shrinking. Instead, the way the business is defined is continually changing.

Those who don't evolve don't make it. It's Darwinism for salespeople, with yesterday's champion becoming today's small flightless bird, smacked in the head by a bat with an Apple logo on the side.

This has consequences for human beings, for delicate measures of company health like morale. If you have to fire good people with every market fluctuation, it becomes very easy to turn your company into a revolving door. Staff don't stay long because they're afraid of being made redundant, and even the few long-termers don't feel much in the way of loyalty (for the same reason). So nobody grows, nobody coheres, nobody fights to make things better. Ultimately, nobody cares.

In our experience, staying small correlates with being nice to people. And being nice to people is as essential as ensuring that credit and debit balance.

KESSELS-
KRAMER

60

IS **WRONG.**

KesselsKramer has a very particular stance on awards: as a rule, we don't enter them. This attitude could be interpreted as aloof, even arrogant – we think we're too good. Perhaps there's something to this. Not a lot, but something. However, there are other reasons why we choose to avoid the red carpet, the complimentary margaritas and the free column inches. Those reasons start when you're five years old.

Our lives are award-based. From elementary school onwards, we're taught to love awards, from trophies designed to motivate you to more subtle marks of validation. From one perspective a smiley face on even the most minor multiplication testis an award, a sign of approval, of status within the group.

By the time most of us are fifteen we have chosen one of two paths: either we get super-competitive. Or we opt out.

Neither option is helpful, especially if you're hoping to become more

creative. You don't come up with great ideas by being a grim, frozen perfectionist. And you don't come up with great ideas by watching Star Trek re-runs all day. (Or if you do, those ideas feature guys with pointy ears in futuristic gymslips.)

The reason why our culture of awards isn't helpful is because it's about being right. The most fashionable right kind of work, with the right sort of art direction and copy, stemming from a carefully constructed, right one-line strategy.

Right limits. Once you're right, you have a solution. All avenues are closed. All bets are off. Pack up, go home, nothing to see, nothing to explore.

Furthermore, right stops you being wrong... and wrong is glorious.

Wrong is where the fun lies. Wrong is what brings your freedom, and joyful work, and stupid ideas ("stupid ideas" being another term for "ideas so fresh we don't know what to make of them").

Wrong is magical and contradictory, because eventually wrong makes a truer form of right. Once every wrong has been fully explored, once all participating minds have been left open for the maximum amount of time, true solutions present themselves. Because these solutions are the result of a non-competitive, collaborative process, everyone involved in the project can hopefully own, support, defend and feel proud of them.

KIK
OUTLET.

KK Outlet is the newest development in the philosophy of staying small in order to experiment more. *fig. 03*

In 2007 KesselsKramer expanded westward by about 370 km, ending up in London's Hoxton Square. Renowned for creativity, innovation and painfully talented young things in equally painful tight jeans, the East End has long been associated with subcultures and fashion (also with extremely unpleasant gangsters — but that was a long time ago).

Here, KK Outlet was born: an ultra-compact space containing a combination of communications agency, gallery and shop.

The communications agency produced communications (unsurprisingly).

The gallery continued KesselsKramer's long tradition of supporting and exhibiting its favourite artists — this time on-site.

And the shop sold KK products, as well as inspiration in the form of

books, magazines and assorted objects that KK staff found worthy of wider attention.

KK Outlet is KesselsKramer's love of diversity incarnate. Over a few brief years it's hosted art openings every few weeks, worked for the biggest of international clients and developed the most small-scale of personal projects.

At least one of which didn't remain small for very long. Stay tuned.

Fig. 03: KK Outlet, KesselsKramer's pocket-sized London-based shop/gallery/ communications agency.

LIBERATION THROUGH DIY.

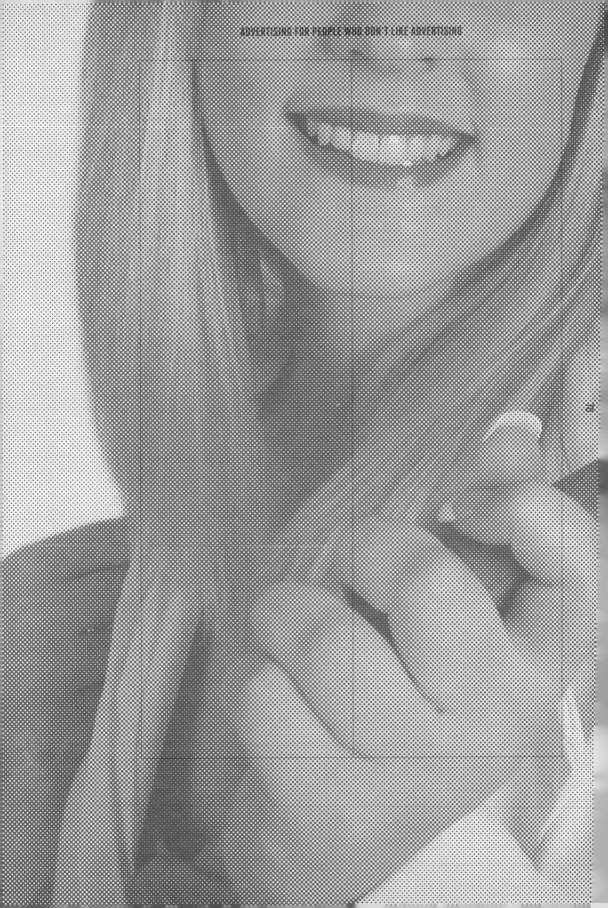

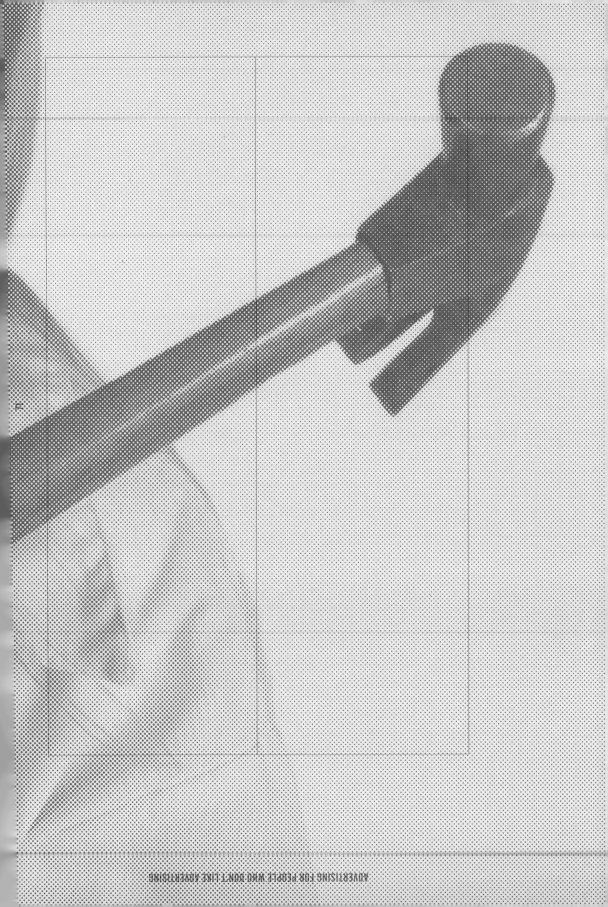

If you're too busy winning, you rarely have time to play. Which is a pity because playing is a way to learn, both for babies and advertising people.

KesselsKramer has long advocated personal projects, the business-usefulness of which is apparent only later, or indirectly.

Over our history we've made photo-graphy magazines, soap, polar bear candles, art exhibitions, puzzles, stickers begging for the end of eighties revivals, books of short stories, more stickers, knitted iPod holders, more stickers, documentary films, music videos, sculptures, architecture and pretty much anything else that might intrigue a creative mind. Including stickers.

We do these things because they're fun, for the sake of it, because they frequently generate PR, and (very straightforwardly) because many of Kessels-Kramer's people are compelled to make stuff.

Beyond this, a personal project can be a mini-university, teaching you skills that can be applied to bigger, more commercial tasks.

At the very least, the process of coming up with an idea, producing that idea and marketing the end result is a massive step toward self-sufficiency. Spend enough passion working on personal projects and you're able to manage yourself — which allows those with the word "manager" on their business cards to stop holding your hand and focus elsewhere.

At most, the output of these mini-universities snowballs into something rather grand. Recently, a self-initiated project in KK Outlet ended up on ABC and other TV stations from Europe to Australia, as well as *Vanity Fair*, *The Daily Telegraph* and assorted legendary publications, some online, some off-.

It started with plates. *fig. 04*

Specifically, it started by printing designs on plates. More specifically still, it started with printing designs on plates to commemorate the English royal wedding of Prince William and his Kate.

Traditionally, patriots and opportunists roll out all kinds of mugs, scarves, clocks, postcards and photography books to accompany British state occasions — enough souvenirs to quench the memorabilia-lust of aunties for the next thousand years.

The peak of this gold-leafed product orgy is the royal wedding, with the loved-up aristocrats plastered onto every available household item. Usually, these objects are nothing if not respectful: the owner swears his allegiance to Queen and country by purchasing a print of a Prince waving from a carriage.

KK Outlet decided to slightly deflate the pomp of this occasion by printing gently ironic messages on dishes. Among them were the sadly reflective: "It Should Have Been Me,"

ATTRACTION: Traders are hoping to cash in on Wills, seen here outside Annabel's members club, in London, yesterday

Picture: OPTICPHOTOS

Tat'll do nicely for my big day

■ by KEIR MUDIE

TRADERS have rushed out an alternative selection of wedding goodies after a ban on tacky official souvenirs for Prince William and Kate's big day.

The pair, both 28, marry on April 29, and the Queen has ensured chances of cashing in will be strictly limited.

Tea-towels have been banned, along with a range of other tacky goods. But plates and china are allowed.

Bender

So the company KK Outlet has launched a range with a difference.

It is offering royal fans a chance to get their hands on a wide selection of souvenir plates.

It includes one thanking the royal pair for a free day off and the chance of a four-day bender.

And there is even a Pearly King Cockney-style plate promising punters a "Right royal knees-up". Another has

FAIR PLATE: Alternative souvenir crockery

a childlike drawing of the couple and the motto: Royal wedding in an age of austerity.

While another one jokes: bigwillie ♥babykins.

Souvenir T-shirts are also on the list as the couple try to keep their wedding tasteful.

A Royal Family spokesman said: "We want items that are permanent and significant."

IT SHOULD HAVE BEEN ME

THANKS FOR THE FREE DAY OFF.

HRH PRINCE WILLIAM & KATE MIDDLETON'S 4 DAY BENDER. 29TH APRIL - 2ND MAY 2011

Fig. 04: KK Outlet's set of plates, designed to celebrate the English royal wedding in mildly ironic fashion. Reports of the plates appeared worldwide.

and a line pin-pointing the true cause for national jubilation: "Thanks For The Free Day Off."

To mark this royal occasion there were more official plates produced than would fill all the dishwashers in the Milky Way. However, the unofficial KK Outlet plates stood out from their china brethren by communicating the opposite of more canonical messages — and quite possibly reflecting what people were thinking but not often saying.

KK Outlet's server crashed due to interest in the ironic plates. Thousands upon thousands were sold and the line was picked up by John Lewis, a national British retail chain.

On the day of the wedding itself, banners of the most popular lines were made and distributed, resulting in a Flickr bomb of images.

It's not that worldwide fame and adulation are necessary results of a self-initiated project, but they do demonstrate a very direct and quantifiable reason to take such projects seriously.

INTERVIEW WITH

ERIK KESSELS.

Erik Kessels is creative director
and co-founder of KesselsKramer.
Here, he talks mobile phones,
bad hotels and pushing boundaries
through collaboration.

MOBILE PHONES FOR A BETTER WORLD.

"As creative people, our job is simple: to search for unused ground… and then use it. This 'unused ground' can be found in execution, in ideas, a certain tone of voice. It's anything that means escaping from the average, from the mainstream.

"You wish you could do it every day, make advertising for people who don't

like advertising, but you can't. At most you find it only a few times a year.

"From our own work, Ben is a good example — a campaign where we found 'unused ground' within the telecommunications category. Not only did we develop the brand name, identity and campaigns, we helped make mobile phones accessible to the majority of people. We positioned Ben as the mobile brand for everyone, from the elderly to migrants to punks to goths. You saw this in the kinds of people used in the campaigns — not traditional models, but people representing these minority groups.

"In fact, Ben became a mirror for Dutch society and hugely popular, especially amongst those who normally never saw people from their subculture in mainstream advertising. fig. 05 What we especially liked about this approach was that it commented indirectly on a great shift in Dutch politics: over the years that we've been running the Ben campaign, the political atmosphere turned from tolerant and progressive to conservative, almost xenophobic. Our client was brave enough

to stick to their guns and celebrate the Netherlands' diversity.

"It would be good if more companies dared to investigate this kind of messaging. Wider cultural concerns are always on their list of values, but you never see them expressed publicly. Just to see these issues addressed in advertising that isn't government funded would be subversive, but subversive with a point, not just for the sake of it."

Fig. 05: Below and following spread: Early work for Ben, a Dutch mobile phone network that sought to humanize a sector dominated by technology-based messages.

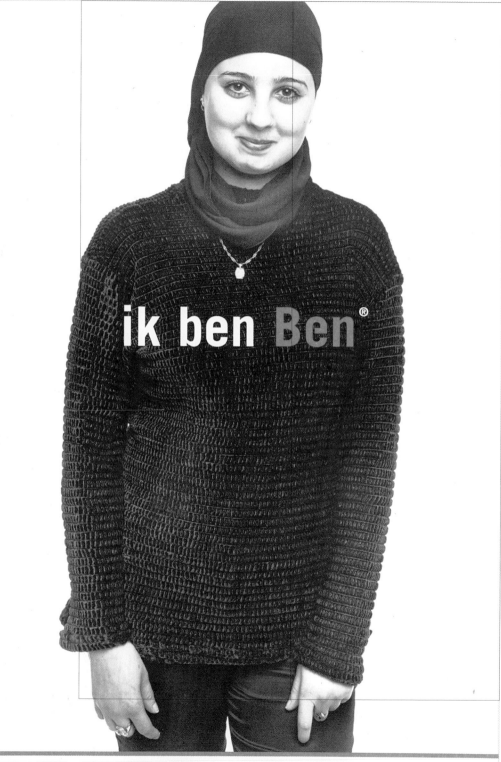

een nieuw mobiel netwerk

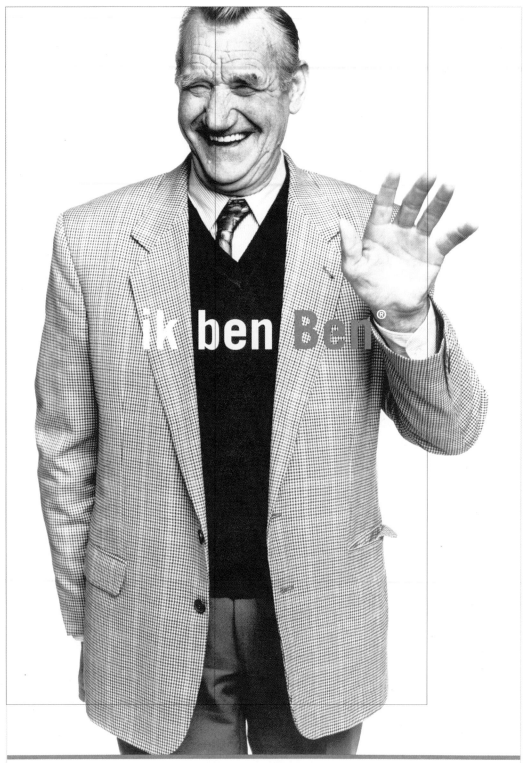

een nieuw mobiel netwerk

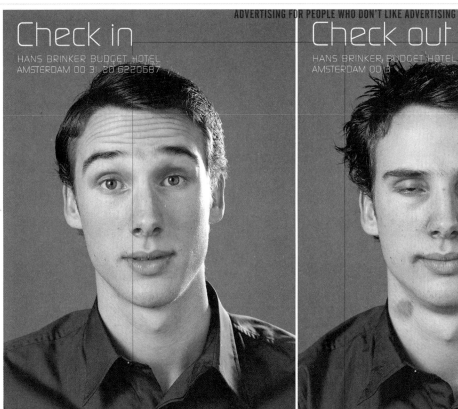

Check in

HANS BRINKER BUDGET HOTEL
AMSTERDAM 00 31 20 6220687

Check out

HANS BRINKER BUDGET HOTEL
AMSTERDAM 00 3

ECO-TOWEL

**HANS
BRINKER
BUDGET
HOTEL.
ACCIDENTALLY
ECO-FRIENDLY.**

KERKSTRAAT 136-138 – AMSTERDAM – TEL +31 (0)20 622 0687 – FAX +31 (0)20 638 2060 – WWW.HANS-BRINKER.COM

THE
WORST
HOTEL IN THE WORLD

UNUSED GROUND AND UNMADE BEDS.

"Another mostly 'unused ground' in advertising is honesty. Absolutely honest ads have appeared every now and again in the industry's history — VW in the sixties being the most famous example. But still, admitting your faults and telling people about your product as straightforwardly as possible is pretty much virgin territory.

"It's an area we like, as probably best demonstrated by our work on KesselsKramer's oldest client: the Hans Brinker Budget Hotel, Amsterdam.

"The Brinker is possibly the worst hotel in the world, a fact we celebrate by describing its many, many faults whenever we can. fig. 06 As a strategy, this isn't as bizarre as it sounds: because we're honest, we get through to the Brinker's young, jaded, suspicious audience. Strangely, by telling people the Brinker is shit, the hotel also gets fewer complaints than you might expect. If a guest knows upfront that they'll get a stained mattress riddled with bedbugs, what else can they bitch about?

"Irony is at the heart of our Brinker work. The most expected way to make advertising for people who don't like advertising is humour. We like funny too, but prefer a more dry, self-referential kind of joke, the sort that you're not sure whether it's serious or not.

"It's not an approach that works for every client, but if taking the piss out of advertising is your thing, fairly sarcastic self-reflexive gags are the way to do it.

"Anti-advertising, I suppose, would be the official term, and the Brinker's a good example."

Fig. 06: Facing page and following spread: Examples of work for the Hans Brinker Budget Hotel. KK's oldest client is famed for its lack of attractive qualities, a fact highlighted in many years of brutally honest campaigns.

IMPROVE YOUR IMMUNE SYSTEM

THE HANS BRINKER BUDGET HOTEL AMSTERDAM   +31 20 622 0687

NOW EVEN MORE DOGSHIT IN THE MAIN ENTRANCE

Hans Brinker Budget Hotel Amsterdam
☎ 31 20 6220687

PERFECT IS BORING.

"You can use advertising as a mirror to consumers, to reflect real lives, but it's an opportunity that is almost always missed.

"Normally we do the opposite. Normally advertising is about making everything 100% perfect. There are no mistakes, everyone and everything is flawless. But it's far more interesting to leave a big mistake in an ad, or to show people who aren't air-brushed and idealized. That way, we recognize ourselves. fig. 07

"Why is there this love of perfection in advertising? Partly it's about fear, about not wanting to offend or alienate people by highlighting the less glossy side of life. It's also because perfection is possible: there's time, money and will to make every-thing flawless. There's total control. Ads are perfectly created from bottom-left to top-right, every detail deliberated over and endlessly polished.

"While working on the Diesel 'Action' campaign, I tried to select images of models where they aren't quite as idealized as you might expect. Perhaps the pose would be slightly 'off' in some way, or the angle not conventionally flattering. By choosing images like these, you make the campaign slightly more authentic."

Fig. 07:

Facing page and next page, left.

Samples of KK's Diesel work.

The Italian brand took a critical

view on the fashion world,

with ads going far beyond the

industry standard images of

pretty people looking seductive.

ACTION!
FOR SUCCESSFUL LIVING

RESPECT YOUR MOM.

protest, support and act at www.diesel.com

DIESEL®
FOR SUCCESSFUL LIVING

SAVE
YOURSELF /
DRINK URINE

Helen Pickering, born 1899

www.diesel.com

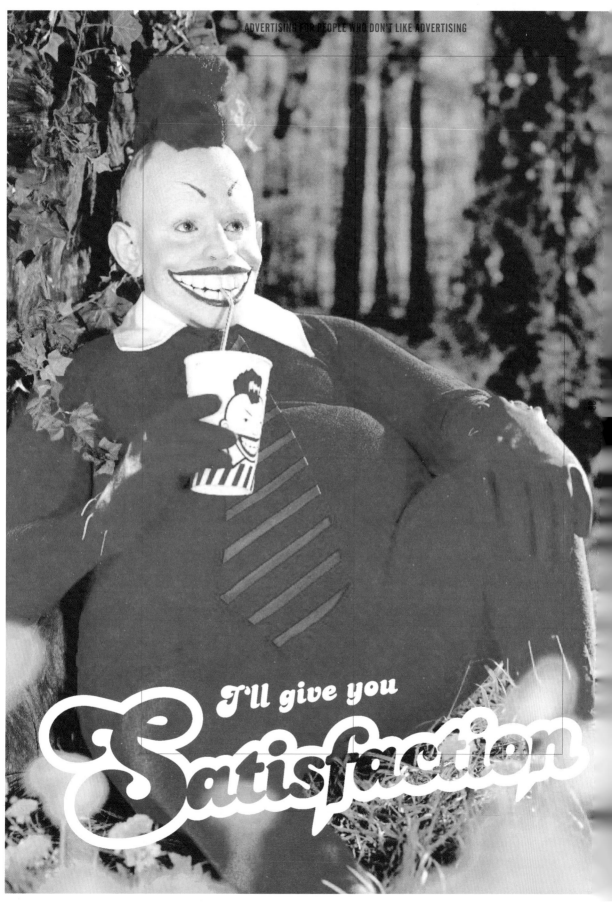

I'll give you
Satisfaction

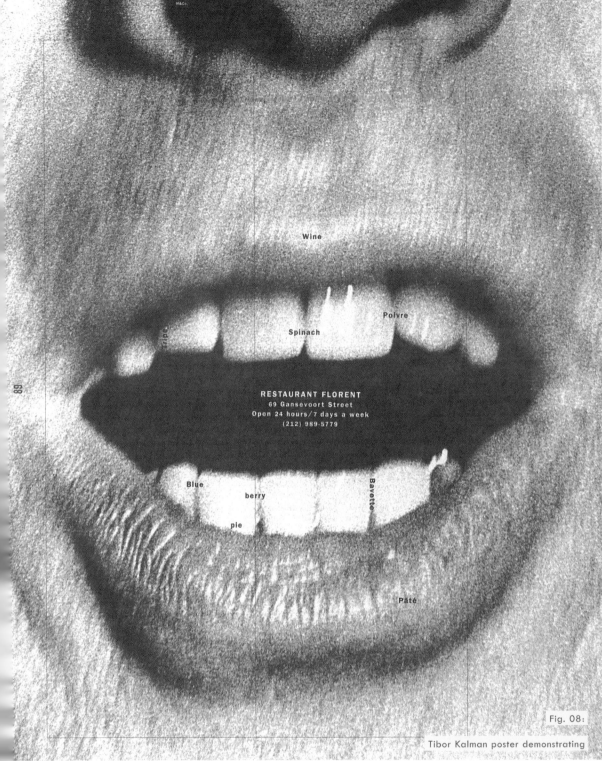

Wine

Poivre

Tripe

Spinach

RESTAURANT FLORENT
69 Gansevoort Street
Open 24 hours / 7 days a week
(212) 989-5779

Blue

berry

pie

Bavette

Pâté

Fig. 08:

Tibor Kalman poster demonstrating

that the convention of "always

be positive" can be broken and still

result in arresting work.

HUNTING FOR AUTHENTIC.

"Avoid getting your inspiration from advertising. In a way, looking to advertising is pointless. If you see a good idea you can admire it, but it wouldn't be wise to re-use it.

"It's better to get your inspiration outside the business. Tibor Kalman is a fine example of someone who did just that. fig. 08 He was prolific in both where he looked for inspiration and what he produced as a result. Kalman made products, books, a magazine and also ads. There you see somebody who is not focused on advertising, and in so doing comes up with much fresher ideas.

"You know you've got it right when you're totally shocked by one of your own ideas. It might happen once or twice a year but it's the best feeling. You think: 'Did I just do that?'"

ON FRESH THINKING THROUGH COLLABORATION.

"I wouldn't go so far as to call this a 'technique' for producing original work, but there's something to be said for collaborating with creatives outside the industry. Industrial designers, photographers, architects and documentary film directors, for instance, who are new to advertising. Often they end up breaking the rules without being aware of those rules in the first place. That's very refreshing.

"This collaboration wasn't always possible. Photography is a case in point. At one time advertising photography was confined to a pool of thirty to forty photographers whom all advertising agencies tended to hire. These photographers were good. In fact, they were master copiers, and by hiring them you were guaranteed a high standard of work. They could do everything, except work in their own style.

"Fairly recently, however, more and more outsider photographers began offering their services. Among them were photojournalists and art photographers interested by the power and reach of commercial work.
If you allow them freedom, and can keep compromises to a minimum, the results are generally great.

"I remember my first experience of working like this. At the time, Johan Kramer and I were still working in London, before we set up KesselsKramer. I'd always admired the work of a photographer called Simon Larbalestier, the man behind The Pixies' album covers. By chance, I came across his portfolio, and ended up hiring him for a job for the British government.

"In the end it worked out well but I was incredibly nervous — which is something you have to deal with if you end up working with those you really admire."

THE COMFORT CONTRADICTION.

"There was a period when I travelled by train every day. After two weeks I started recognizing my fellow passengers and began to feel stuck in a routine. From then on I'd find different ways to enter the station, and different places to stand on the platform, all in order to avoid coming across the same people in the morning. The urge to break these little habits is something I experience quite a lot.

"Getting too comfortable isn't good. Comfort is what people naturally seek, but if we want to stay true to our desire to produce the best work, it's best avoided. It means you stop questioning.

"Mind you, it's probably good to qualify this a bit. You also need to have certain desires met before you get the luxury of restlessly questioning everything. If you look at the countries with the very highest creative output, you also see the very highest levels of material comfort.

The Scandinavian countries or Switzerland are prime examples.

"In these places there's a certain feeling of fulfilment on a societal level that perhaps leads to boredom at the level of individuals. You get so comfortable that at some point you become uncomfortable again. Then you start making great work.

"Maybe it goes back to Abraham Maslow's hierarchy of needs: once you have the basics, it's easier to focus on stuff like creativity, being tolerant and other values we tend to admire."

KESSELSKRAMER PUBLISHING.

"No matter how many gadgets, widgets and e-readers come out, books seem to remain special to people. It's like loving books is wired into people's brains.

"As a company, we've always been interested in storytelling for brands, so storytelling through books seemed like a logical step. fig. 09

"Our publishing arm, KesselsKramer Publishing, was created to provide a means for KesselsKramer's staff to express their creativity through pictures, words and any combination of the two.

"The books we make are treated as interesting objects in their own right, not just a medium for conveying information and ideas. We use all kinds of unusual paper, new types of binding and formats.

"A large part of KK Publishing's output is in the field of found photography. Also called 'the people's camera' or

'vernacular photography,' this area is about collecting and presenting images never intended for public display.

"It's the opposite of most advertising photography, which is almost exclusively concerned with picture manipulation and very definite agendas.

"The style of KK Publishing's books filters back into KK's commercial ventures, inspiring us to find the most genuine, most human side of advertising photography."

Fig. 09:

Examples from KK Publishing,
demonstrating an output that
includes magazines, photography
books and fiction.

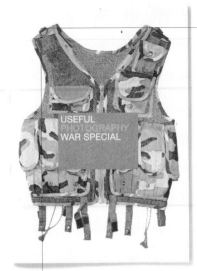

USEFUL
PHOTOGRAPHY
WAR SPECIAL

USEFUL
PHOTOGRAPHY
004

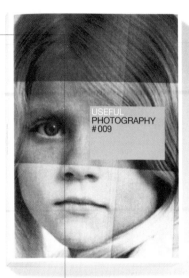

USEFUL
PHOTOGRAPHY
009

USEFUL
PHOTOGRAPHY
#001

USEFUL
PHOTOGRAPHY
008

USEFUL
PHOTOGRAPHY
007

USEFUL
PHOTOGRAPHY
006

USEFUL
PHOTOGRAPHY
002

ADVERTIS-ING FROM THE

96

OUTSIDE: INTERVIEW

WITH STEFAN SAGMEISTER.

Stefan Sagmeister is a Grammy award-winning designer. He's created album covers for The Rolling Stones, Lou Reed and David Byrne. Other clients include HBO and the Guggenheim Museum. Here, he discusses advertising from a design perspective, sabbaticals and what creative responsibility means to him.

ON ADS AND ATTITUDES.

"I ran Leo Burnett's design studio in Hong Kong for about six months. After that, I switched to advertising within Burnett's, expecting not to like it, and finding that expectation to be true.

"Hong Kong at that time was an incredibly dense and booming market. It was here that I encountered a behaviour that I've noticed at many agencies around the world: there's too much turning of the

wheel and much too little thinking. This applies to both agencies and their clients. Both parties come up with an idea and immediately say: let's do it. Nobody pauses to ask the proper questions or wonder whether what they're doing is worth doing. After this initial approval of the idea, there's an unreasonable amount of time spent on revising, revising and revising again.

"This questionable process leads to dubious work. There's not much advertising that makes my day. Having said this, there are very rare moments when I see an unbelievable creative peak. When these occur they become part of culture. Examples are the first Sony Bravia TV spot, *fig. 10* or certain pieces of Nike work that I just really love as pieces of popular culture.

"These things exist because an advertiser paid for them, of course, and that money can be a force for good. Advertising is what allows *The New York Times* to exist, for instance. Without advertising, its quality would go down, or it would cease entirely.

"The fact is that good work requires an unbelievable amount of discipline. If the conditions in a place of work are terrible, then good work is almost impossible to realize. In most ad agencies good conditions don't exist so good work doesn't either.

"I remember this from a company like Leo Burnett, but it's also something

Fig. 10:

"An unbelievable creative peak." Sony Bravia's TV spot, one of the very few ads to get the Sagmeister stamp of approval.

66

I see reflected in friends of mine —
people who work in agencies, but all
their time is soaked up in meetings,
so much so that there's no time left to
come up with good concepts.

"Because these people are working under
pressure, they frequently pick ideas from
others without crediting them. It's not that
they're bad people — I do think that the
problems are much more systemic than
personal. The advertising system does little
to bring out the best in people.

"I've had friends who took an ad
agency job for three years, and in those
three years they behaved like assholes.
They behaved terribly, not returning phone
calls, asking others to work for free, and
after six months of free work turning
around and saying that the concept has
been killed. Then they quit their jobs, left
the system, and were perfectly fine again.

"I'm not sure where this rudeness comes
from, because it's been a while since I've
worked in ad agencies myself.
But time constraints are a part of it.
I remember from my own career,

I once worked on a project for an airline
company, but the time I actually spent on
the creation of that campaign might have
been 3%. Everything else was meetings,
revisions, plans being changed, and
meetings to prevent the changing of
those plans."

SELLING IS WHAT WE DO.

"Ultimately, advertising is selling. My
parents were salespeople, so selling in
and of itself is not a problem for me.
Ultimately, selling is merely the exchange
of goods or ideas, and that's fundamen-
tally human.

"I'd improve the state of advertising
through a few simple adjustments.
Firstly, I'd follow São Paulo's lead. Here,
they removed all outdoor advertising.
Wherever there was a billboard, now
there's just space, fig. 11 and for me that's
a clear improvement. There's just no more
ugly crap hanging around.

"I spent a lot of time in Indonesia, and that's the opposite extreme. There you can see how badly they need such regulations. Thanks to small shops with laser printers, everyone's able to produce very cheap banners. As a result, every possible inch of space is filled with these ugly ads. They are everywhere: in the jungle or next to a remote road.

"I think that one reason the quality of communication is so low in such places is this lack of restrictions. With more restrictions you force people to be clever, to use creativity in order to work around legal impingements."

adolescent. Through this overexposure, happiness becomes completely meaningless to the consumer. fig. 12 If you see a happy face on a pack shot, it's unlikely you'll believe that the product will make you happier."

One of Stefan Sagmeister's life lessons, published in his book *Things I Have Learned In My Life So Far.*

THE CYNICAL BUSINESS OF HAPPINESS.

"Advertising treats happiness very cynically. In commercials, it's almost impossible to represent happiness honestly, because it's been used over and over again, endlessly. Every brochure features some sort of happy couple, or a smiling baby or

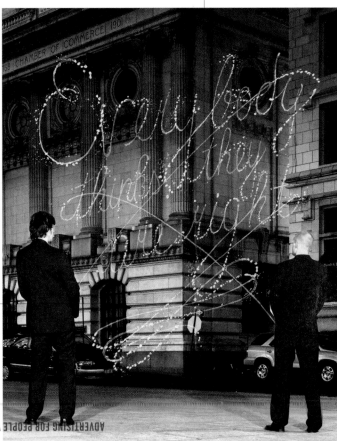

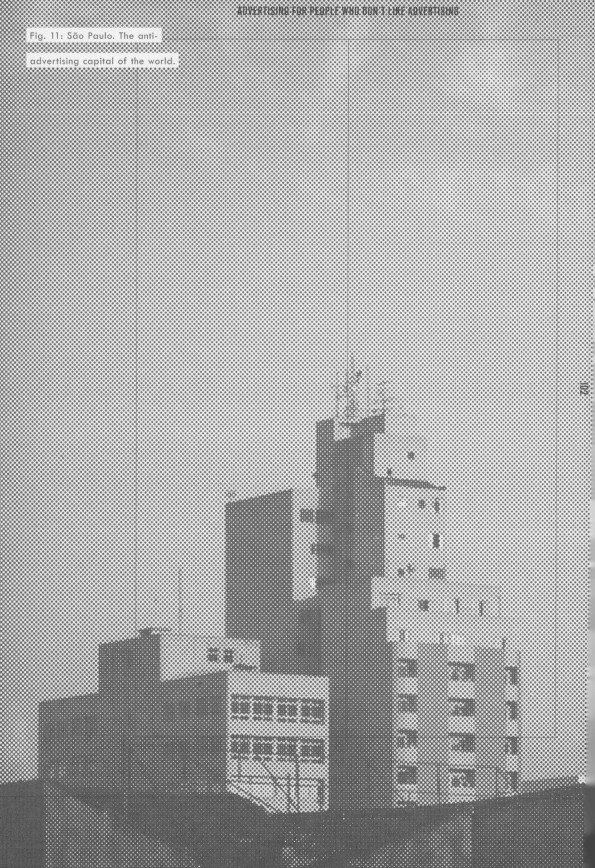

Fig. 11: São Paulo. The anti-
advertising capital of the world.

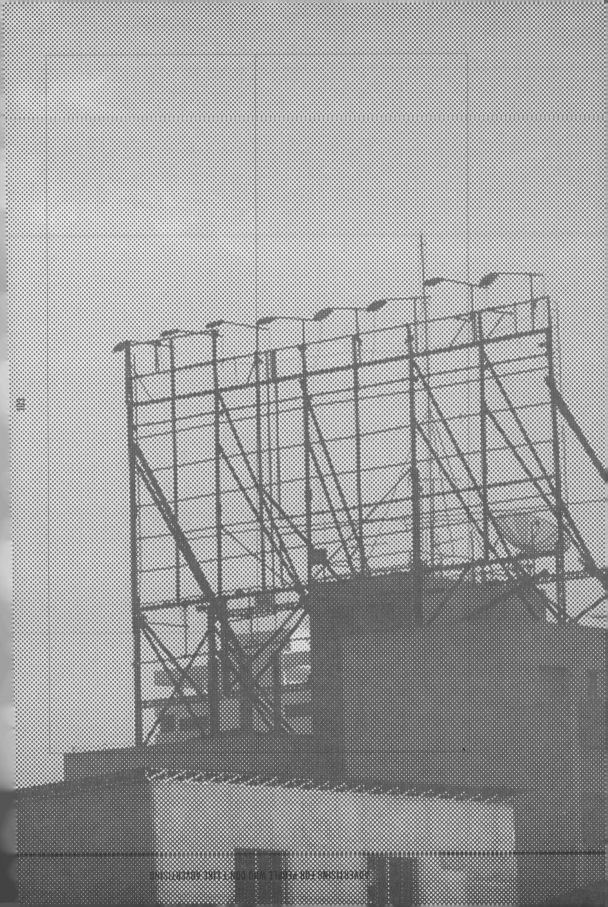

ANXIETY AND CREATIVITY.

"My least favourite part of the creative process is anxiety. But I do believe it to be necessary. If your desire is to create something new, something you haven't done before, then anxiety will be a component.

"But while you probably can't do without a measure of anxiety, we try to limit it. Here in my studio we try to keep anxiety in check by setting very generous deadlines."

CLIENTS TO AVOID.

"If a client approaches us and says: 'We need something next week' then we don't take that client. It's not because we don't want to work on something that has to be finished next week. It's because a client who comes in that late gives the impression that he's disorganized, and that will lead to future problems. My least favourite client is a disorganized one."

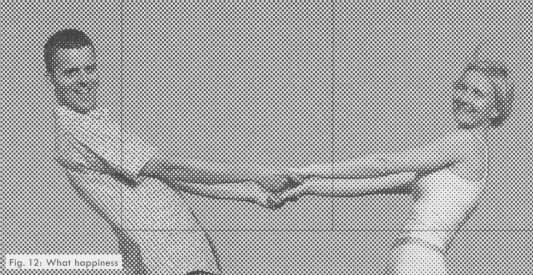

Fig. 12: What happiness looks like, apparently. Some overly used shots of overly smiley people.

SOCIAL
AND
CREATIVE
RESPONSIBILITY.

"Of the work that we've done, there's one socially responsible campaign that I'm happiest with, and that's the mobile money campaign. It was about trying to change the United States government's attitude to poverty by cutting the military budget, and spending more money on education instead. fig. 13

"I like it, but it's hard to gauge its success because the Obama administration also implemented similar measures. So I can't really claim a direct effect but it definitely did something. We gained an unbelievable 800,000 members within six months.

"We've just been involved with an organization that makes products by asking factions in warzones to collaborate. For instance, asking Israelis and Palestinians to work together, or Pakistanis and Indians, and so on. We did a couple of presentations for them, so it's early stages.

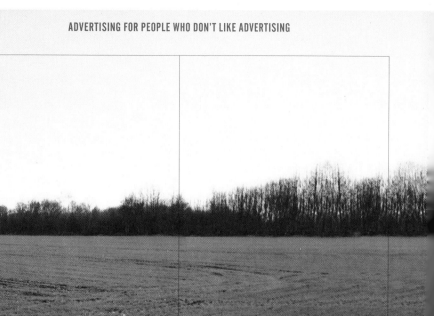

Fig. 13:

Guns don't kill people, governments do. Sagmeister visualizes the vast sums of money spent by very large countries to guard against a negligible threat.

"In the end, working for NGOs is really, really difficult. Small NGOs have the disadvantage of only being able to do small things. Really large NGOs have the disadvantage of having boards, which means having to get everything approved by that board.

"At one point, I was actually playing with this idea of only accepting socially responsible jobs. But in the end, this doesn't work financially.

"The furthest I've ever been down this path is when we tried to set up our own charity. I wondered whether I should really remain a designer, or switch to the charity sector.

"Ultimately charity work is un-believably difficult, though. I was pretty mediocre at running a charity, so I stayed with design.

"Overall what is best is working with an NGO in a particular way, to the extent that we really become part of that organization before we even start the project.

In this way, we get to know them from inside.

"If you want to make a socially responsible piece of communication that actually works and has a result, it has to be pure. If I look at the award books and see all the social responsibility ads, I see only a motivation to win prizes. There's no genuine desire to generate serious results for the client.

"From a creative point of view, I would divide advertising into three groups. The first group comprises the vast majority of what we actually see out there on the streets, or on radio and TV. This is the stuff I'd class as simply terrible. It's also the main reason I'd rather not watch TV or listen to the radio.

"The second group is the award-winning stuff. It's very clever and wonderful, but ultimately has been made only to advance one's career. It doesn't actually have a function or sell a product. This work is made by grown men and women actually spending serious

time and effort to gain a little trophy.

The biggest joke is that it isn't even real. When I judged an ad competition in Asia a few years ago the co-judges told me 80% of all the ads were fake.

"That leaves the third and very small category of excellent work for real clients. And that stuff is unbelievably difficult to do. The people who actually make campaigns that work for clients — selling a product or spreading a message, or raising money for a charity — are fantastic. But they're only a tiny percentage."

Fig. 14: Talkative Chair.
The text refers to a diary entry
Sagmeister wrote while sitting
on the balcony in Bali where the
finished chair would be placed.

BETTER WORKING BY NOT WORKING.

"I take one year off every seven years in order to go on a working sabbatical. During that time I stop working for my regular clients, go off and experiment, try out other things.

"I've done two so far in my studio. The first one was in 2000 and led to work that I was really happy with, and still am. A lot of work that we've made after the sabbatical was somehow influenced by that period. fig. 14

"Sabbaticals really get more out of you as a designer. I think partly because many people coming out of design school see design as their calling, and that narrowness of focus can limit you. They get used to the stuff that they like, and they get bored of it as well. A working sabbatical helps in getting to know what you like or are good at, next to your daily work.

"Perhaps unexpectedly, the most common reaction I get from clients to taking the sabbatical isn't resistance. It's more likely to be: 'My God, I would love to do that.'

"Sabbaticals are about stepping outside routines. They're not about working hard because everybody else is working hard. They're more about what works for you."

Sagmeister's billboard for Experimenta, Lisbon. The text is made from newsprint, which fades in sunlight. Over time the message (and the complaining) disappears.

ADVICE FOR WORKING LIFE.

"There's a book by the philosopher Alain de Botton called The Pleasures and Sorrows of Work. In it he asks: 'When will we perceive our work to be meaningful?' He answers this with a single sentence: 'When it delights people or when it helps people.'

"And I think this line clearly applies to advertising. If you look at the people who have been in advertising for a long time and are still engaged in what they do, you see that they are interested in delighting or helping people, or a mixture of both."

Sagmeister's sage words: "Money does not make me happy," spelled out here in graphic form as part of his book *Things I Have Learned In My Life So Far.*

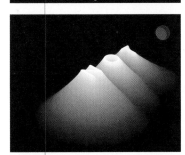

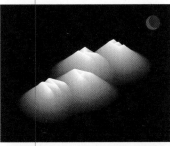

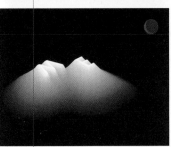

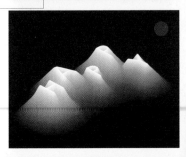

113

ALEX BOGUSKY'S REMORA ON THE

UNDER-BELLY OF CAPITALISM

Alex Bogusky was creative director of advertising agency Crispin Porter + Bogusky. He has been named Creative Director of the Decade, inaugurated into the American Advertising Federation's Hall of Achievement and received an honorary PhD from the University of Colorado. In 2010 he retired from advertising in order to aid the "new consumer revolution" from his base, the Fearless Cottage.

THE BACKGROUND OF BOGUSKY.

"I grew up in a family of graphic designers. I didn't go to college and I didn't have any particular drive except that I tried to become a professional motocrosser for a while. And when that fell through I settled back into graphics because that was all I knew.

"And through graphics I accidentally wound up working in an advertising

agency. I had never really considered advertising or thought about it, but there I was. The agency wasn't very good so I still didn't think that the industry was all that great either.

"I remember that one of the art directors had a bunch of annuals. I was used to design annuals because that was the world I came from, but I'd never seen a One Show or anything like that. So I started looking at that work and I realized that there are people who are really good at this, and the way they do it is really fun, really creative, and I wanted to do that.

"So I started messing around on my own, trying out that kind of advertising, and it wasn't well received at the agency. Luckily, I'd known Chuck Porter for a while. He was working as a copywriter and he eventually hired me, thinking that what I was doing was pretty cool."

RESPECT THE PEOPLE, NOT THE FORM.

"I once told a reporter that I had no respect for advertising, and his face fell. He was really upset by those words. I realized that the way he took it was different to how I had meant it. I have respect for the people and I have respect for what's been done, I just didn't think the form was about respect. I thought it was much more about recreating and reinventing.

"For me, you can be frozen if you idolize something. You can have so much respect for the work that has been done before that it's impossible to take the form forwards. I had to not respect it in order to move it.

"And of course, there's a lot that's awful, but it can be awful in different ways. It can be awful in ways that are benign, but it can also be awful in ways that are really malevolent.

"I think that if you're mindful and you work in the business you're just worried about what it is you do. There's the fact that sometimes you can hurt people and ideas and culture, and that's balanced by the fact that you really get off on manipulating culture. There's this high you get, similar to the rush a musician or a celebrity gets from playing within pop culture. You get that same high from behind the scenes."

HOW TO SLEEP AT NIGHT.

"The question of ethics in advertising is huge.

"I think that there are broader, more accepted cultural ethics, and advertising as an industry generally plays within the boundaries of those. You don't see it move outside of this ethical system, and that's why it's an accepted cultural form.

"But then there are also people's individual ethics and morals. As you work in the business, those ethics and morals may come into conflict with things that you are asked to do. At that point you can take one of two positions. Some people ignore their own personal ethics. They think: 'I don't have the power to say no to this, this is my job.' I hear that stance a lot.

"Other people speak up. Probably they sometimes get fired, but at other times they get heard.

"I never had a problem with people saying: 'I won't work on this.' There's always lots of other stuff to work on. I have good friends who wouldn't work on alcohol, and that was fine. And I've had Mormons who won't drink alcohol, but will work on alcohol. Also fine. Those are personal ethical questions."

SEX AND ADVERTISING.

"Is advertising inherently unethical? Or when does it become unethical? It's like asking: is sex unethical?

"It's not. It depends on how you treat it.

"And advertising, in its purest form, is getting attention. Is it unethical to get attention for something? No.

"I think we can probably all agree on that. Is it unethical to get attention for some things? Probably.

"I do think that our larger cultural morals and values could be equated to the seven deadly sins. I'm not a Bible-thumping evangelist, but if you look at where those sins come from, they're probably guides for society as well as religion. They were probably guidelines for happiness.

"And advertising generally works against those guidelines. Lust, envy, gluttony and the rest can all be seen in advertising's

mainstream — you can identify those ideas through the majority of work. So just by having messages present that promote these things would be for some, I would say, an unethical use of advertising.

"In the business we call it 'aspiration.' It's the basest form of advertising, the one that the bigger clients usually want to push you into. 'Aspiration' is a more palatable word for promoting lust, gluttony, greed, envy, pride. So when you stoke the fires of those things in a culture, it's not something that feels good.

"There are ways not to do it. I mean, you can definitely use advertising in ways that are more honest, and humorous and insightful. You can make advertising that allows and encourages a totally different kind of behaviour. You can encourage sharing. You can encourage friendliness. You can encourage all sorts of stuff, but instead 'aspiration' seems to be the default setting for your average advertising out there."

POSITIVE ADVERTISING IN PRACTICE.

"I found that you don't have to use this default set of values we call 'aspiration.' The place where I had the most success in putting other ideals into the work was when we introduced Mini Cooper. We did a lot of work about being good to each other on the road. We included messages on road rage, waving to other Mini drivers and helping each other. It was this idea of there being a higher calling for driving, and it worked like crazy. We never did any work that said 'This other guy got the Mini, and you didn't' which is the default message for a lot of automotive advertising, and a lot of beer advertising too.

"For me, it was always fun to find ways of weaving these messages into the work that we were doing. The way I looked at it is: you have millions of dollars funding this loudspeaker that can shout into culture. Yeah, you were charged with selling this

product. But what else was going to be in that communication? It could be anything. So it was always fun and a bit of a puzzle to try to inject something that we felt could be good for people to hear.

"When we launched Microsoft the campaign was based on connection, and the fact that that we're all connected. I got Deepak Chopra in the spots and I'd written his script: this is Deepak and this is what I think he's going to say. We got a response, which was: 'Deepak wants to do it but he wants to write his own thing,' and people were worried I'd be offended. And I'm like 'Whatever. Trust me, whatever he writes is going to be perfect.' And it was.

"Generally, though, I was never very successful at getting other people to like this game of using advertising as a vehicle for bigger values. One reason was that many people I worked with just weren't into it. Perhaps they were just too worried about getting the work done, period. They didn't have time or energy to inject that kind of thinking into whatever campaign we were producing. But that's okay. You can't really expect advertising to be an especially enlightened industry within an unenlightened society.

"Advertising is definitely a reflection of society. Ultimately, you're nothing more than a list of your clients. You'd like to be more, but the company you keep defines you. I describe advertising as a remora, a sucker fish, on the underbelly of capitalism. It's a parasitic relationship we have with the system as a whole. I think you could remove advertising and the foundation of capitalism would not crumble."

MAKE
A
LIST.

"I don't know if it matters in what way you look outside advertising, but it is important to do so. It's also good to look into the ways in which what we do is criticized. It's easy to close yourself off to the criticism but I try to be pretty open to it. We would have a lot of conversations in the agency where we reflected on what we were doing, asking 'Is this right? Is this wrong?'

"Having said that, when you're in the middle of a situation, a certain amount of your decisions are simply rationalizations. I think that's just very difficult to avoid. So you just have to be diligent, and critical.

"We were having these conversations my whole career. So, early on, I made a list. I encourage people to do this: if you go into advertising, have a list of what you will and won't work on. When I started, the biggest topic was: would you work on tobacco?

"And I honestly would have worked on tobacco. I was pretty laissez-faire, but I was totally unaware of what had gone on in that industry. Once I knew, I could never work on it.

"I added another category that I would never work on, which is advertising to children. Through our work on 'The Truth' anti-tobacco campaign, we learned a lot about tobacco tactics and targeting kids. But we also learned a lot about how a child's brain develops, and in my opinion it's unethical to advertise to children from an adult point of view and with an adult voice, with all these sophisticated tools we have.

"I couldn't do kids advertising once I realized that kids literally haven't developed part of their brain, the part that allows them to see messages as not absolutes. So they really see things in very black and white terms. Whether you're a toy manufacturer, or you make cereals, or whatever, I wouldn't promote your product.

"So that was another category added to my list. Then there was pharmaceuticals. I felt I didn't know enough about how they worked and their side effects to be comfortable working in that area.

"You develop this over your career, and I think everyone should constantly be examining what they will and won't work on.

"Ask yourself: what kind of communication do you feel okay about? Do you feel okay about sharing what this product does? Do you feel okay suggesting to people that if they don't buy this product then they're not cool?"

THE BURGER DILEMMA.

"We asked ourselves these questions when we were working on Burger King. Is it ethical to advertise fast food? Is that something that you feel comfortable with? At the time, I absolutely did. I grew up on fast food, almost exclusively. To me it was an issue of portion control, and not the food itself.

"Today, I would be in a slightly different position because the industrialized food supply has changed what a burger is. It's not the same food I was eating as a kid. I was unaware of this, so I continued working on Burger King, but as I became aware of the processes behind fast food, it started to become a problem for me.

"I think that the more you know, the more you realize that you don't have the whole world to choose from. But that isn't bad. Anybody in advertising or business knows that focusing is the greatest asset you can have. If you can focus your attention and

your talents, you can achieve far more.

So the fact that there are categories beyond where you're willing to go is fine. I had more categories outside of what I was willing to work on than most. There would be all sorts of stuff that we'd be asked to pitch on, and I would say, 'No, we don't do that.' It didn't hamper me. There's plenty out there."

IS ADVERTISING IMPROVING?

"It has the opportunity to get better. I grew up with the notion of parity product marketing, meaning two products that are essentially identical competing against each other — the most famous example being Coke and Pepsi. Back then, the marketer's job was to come up with a story, a reason that made one product seem more appealing than the other. Really this came down to: which product's lie is better? Or which product's lie is more romantic?

"I think this façade of a romantic lie existed on most brands. But these façades are going to have to be replaced. The story is going to be replaced by real-time facts. It's going to happen gradually, but it's going to happen through social media and other tools that people use to access brands.

"Successful brands are beginning to shift from the notion of a story, to working on delivering real-time understanding of

them as a company to consumers. And whoever does that fast gets the biggest brand bump. I think that's a huge and fundamental shift.

"Over the next few years we'll see both versions of branding occurring. There's a lot of old-school branding still going on, and then there's the beginnings of a new and very progressive understanding of branding, based around transparency — if you want to use that term.

"Some of the tools are already there for consumers to be empowered in this way. Some are being created by the brands themselves, and more will come online. This movement isn't exclusive to social media either, unless you include services like WikiLeaks in social media.

"We're seeing the gradual removal of an asymmetry of information that exists in the current state. At the moment, the company has always known more than the consumer. Within companies they have lots of discussions about what consumers can and can't know. This isn't sinister, by the way. It's more about

asking, 'Well, what would be good for consumers to know?'

"That asymmetry is declining because all the information is going to be out there, and everyone will have immediate access to it. Actually, you could viably suggest that the information is already there. The only thing that's missing is more tools with which to access it.

"What I don't know is whether consumers are going to be as involved in this process as they should be in order to have that asymmetry of information disappear in each and every interaction. But it probably doesn't matter because in the aggregate there will be enough consumers that will want it to disappear, enough so that they actually create information equality for the rest."

COMMON.

"I'm troubled by the systemic problems that exist in capitalism now. A lot of people are nostalgic about a time when the government had a stronger role in controlling corporations, but that time is very much gone. Corporations are firmly in control.

"However, I don't think they're sinister. I've met very few evil capitalists. Mostly, they're just really good people. But the system creates a kind of behaviour that will be really damaging for society if left unchanged. I think we're beginning to see that already. There's plenty of proof everywhere.

"Some would look to government to create guidelines, new forms of regulation. I'm sceptical as to whether that's possible given our political system and how much corporate involvement there is in it, via donations, lobbyists, etcetera.

"There are four lobbyists for each member of Congress, and that's just for oil and coal. When you pit that kind of power against my measly vote, my vote doesn't stand a chance. It just doesn't — no rational person can think that their vote is actually going to work.

"We probably won't see any reforms around special interests, since those special interests won't allow that kind of reform. So that isn't a solution.

"Which makes me look to capitalism itself, knowing that the people involved are all really good people, and knowing that it is the most powerful force on Earth. So why fight it? Why not work within it?

"The notion of 'Common' is inspired by a new branch of thought within corporate America. It's tiny but it's there, this idea of the social enterprise. fig. 15

"Historically, corporations had to have a social benefit. This function no longer exists today. The original charters were given only if a social benefit was part of how you proposed to work.

"We're seeing a little of this thinking again. There are social entrepreneurs

creating businesses that do social good by the very way they operate. For me, these social enterprises have the potential to infect lots of other businesses. These social ideas, though they may be small now, could spread to change capitalism as a whole, changing the way that all these good people look at their own companies, and their own role within those companies, and how those companies operate within society.

"My favourite example of this is Patagonia, a real bunch of pioneers. You could describe this as a triple bottom-line company for sure: one that measures profits not just by pure economics, but also by the social and ecological impacts of its product. They would, for sure, fall under conscious capitalism.

"When Walmart decided that they wanted to improve their sustainability index and supply chain, they called in Patagonia. It's just such a great example: Patagonia is a decent-sized company, but it doesn't have Walmart's impact. After all, Walmart is a company so big that it constitutes the nineteenth-largest economy on Earth. So when Walmart looks to little Patagonia for inspiration and direction, it thrills me, honestly, because it shows that capitalism's problems can be fixed from within. It shows that good people are going to pick up on good ideas. We just need to make more partnerships like this.

"Which is where Common comes in. Common wants to create a system to fast-prototype lots of social ventures, and to help social entrepreneurs on their journey. And there will be a community around that, which we've begun at www.common.is.

"We've begun projects, events and launches and all of that comes under the umbrella of Common and the idea of the Common brand, which is: the first collaborative brand.

"We think that social ventures could actually benefit from collaborating with a shared brand that has shared values. Consumers can say: 'If I see Common, I know it represents triple bottom-line,

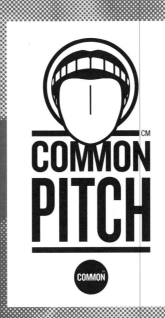

Bogusky's latest project, post-advertising. Under the banner "Common," Alex and his partners seek to update capitalism, and make it a little more pleasant to be around.

COMMON CYCLES

COMMON WATER

COMMON HOME

I know it represents a social venture,
so I feel good about that.'

"Partly we're inspired by companies like
Virgin, which is a unique brand in that
it isn't vertical. Almost all brands are very
vertical. They represent a category.
Virgin's brand represents a set of ideals,
and most of those ideals are based
around having a good time. But they've
been able to move those ideals across
three hundred different companies.
I hadn't even realized it was that many.

"So we want to create a brand that
similarly represents an ideal instead of
a category, but this ideal is the social
venture and the integrated bottom
line. Then we move that across three
hundred or a thousand verticles.
We're pretty excited."

131

ANTHONY BURRILL

IN PICTURES.

Anthony Burrill's iconic posters and designs for brands like Diesel and the Hans Brinker have become recognized worldwide. His work has also appeared in Tate Modern and the Barbican, London. Here, he gives us visual answers to questions about communications.

HOW WOULD YOU DEFINE ADVERTIS-ING?

BUY THIS NOW*

*YOU DON'T NEED THIS

WHY DON'T YOU LIKE ADVERTISING?

READ
ANSWER
ON P.135

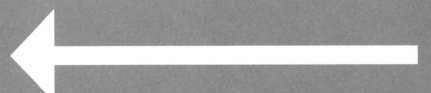

WHAT WOULD MAKE ADVERTIS-ING MORE LIKEABLE FOR YOU?

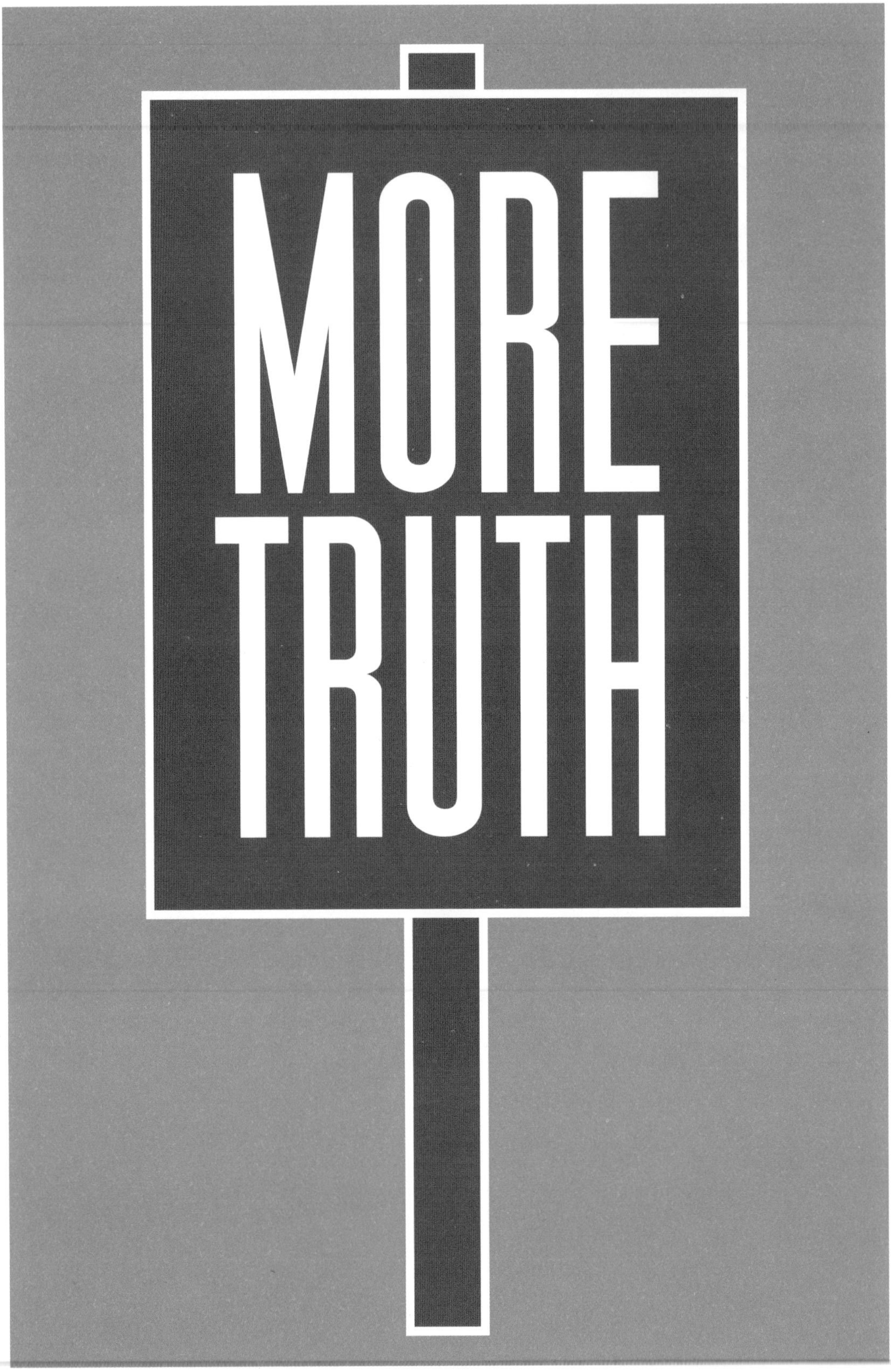
MORE
TRUTH

ARE THERE ANY ADS YOU DO LIKE?

WHAT DO YOU THINK?

WHAT WOULD A WORLD WITHOUT ADS BE LIKE?

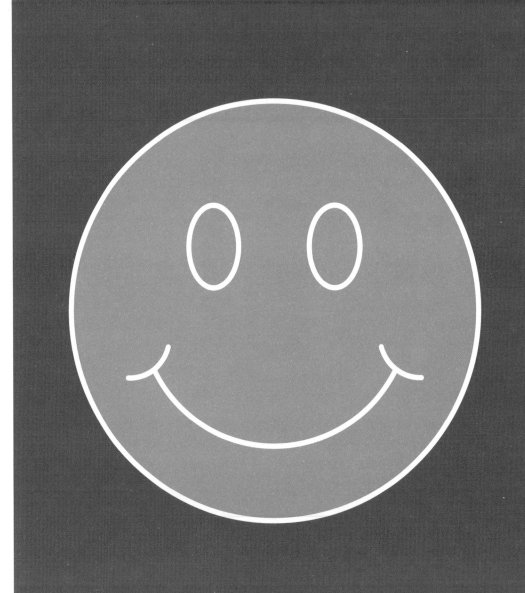

HANS AARSMAN'S HISTORY

OF THE PRESENT.

Hans Aarsman is a photographer, novelist, playwright, curator and journalist. He's also lectured widely at various universities and events, including TED (Technology, Entertainment & Design). For Dutch broadsheet *De Volkskrant*, he writes a popular weekly column on news photography, conducting a detective-likeinvestigation into a particular news photograph, its hidden agendas and how it came to be constructed.

Here, he discusses the points where news meets advertising, advertising photography versus news photography, the power of media and which ads work for him.

BACKGROUND.

"At university I began studying physics and chemistry. After three years you have a practice exam and then you continue, working in laboratories. I was not interested at that point. I thought it was so boring. What we studied was a very small detail of another thing that was also a detail of yet another bigger thing. It was all details and you lost the big picture. So I quit.

"I started to study the Dutch language and literature. Linguistics. I graduated and taught for one or two years at schools before realizing that this was also not something I wanted to go on with. And then I discovered photography. I made my own reportage photos and tried to sell them to the newspapers. It finally worked, so I became a photojournalist.

"I like photography because it's very practical. It's about a machine and equipment that you have to get used to. You have to be handy and quick. It's also a way of expressing yourself but it's not too poetic. I liked journalism because media for me is like the history of now. It's the history of the present.

"But after a few years I discovered this recurring structure in photojournalism. This is the conflict structure — there's always this almost biblical conflict between good and evil. In most newspaper images you'll see one side opposing another, whether those sides are protestors, politicians, or soldiers. So I got bored with that too. I thought, 'That's not the way I want to look at the world.' For me, the world's about much more than black-and-white conflict. It's more versatile and paradoxical.

"So I bought a camper van and I went through Holland taking pictures, trying to take photographs that weren't constrained by form. fig. 16 Just to find another way of looking at things, trying to find my own style of photography.

"I made a book of the camper trip images and realized that these were form-based too. I thought, 'I should stop with photography because it's too much form.'

147

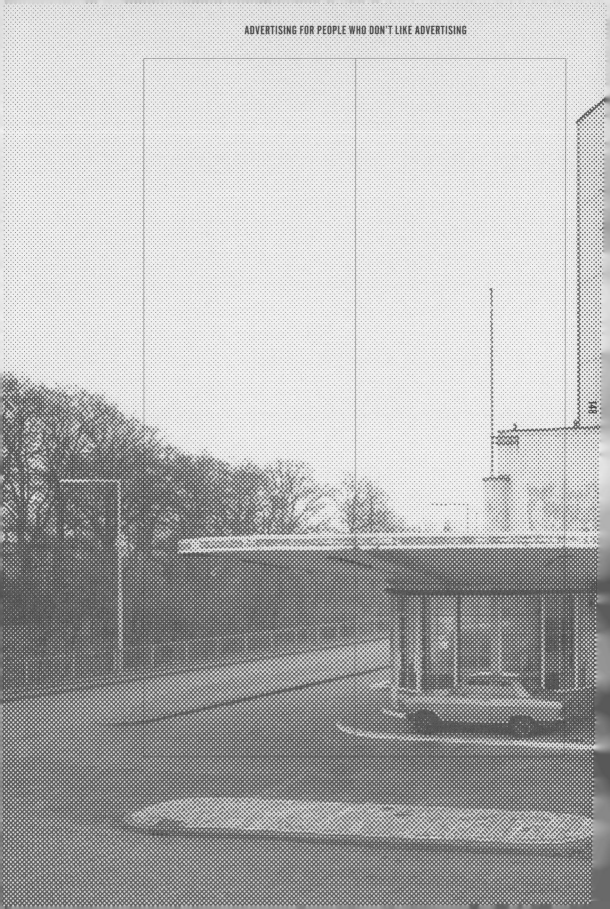

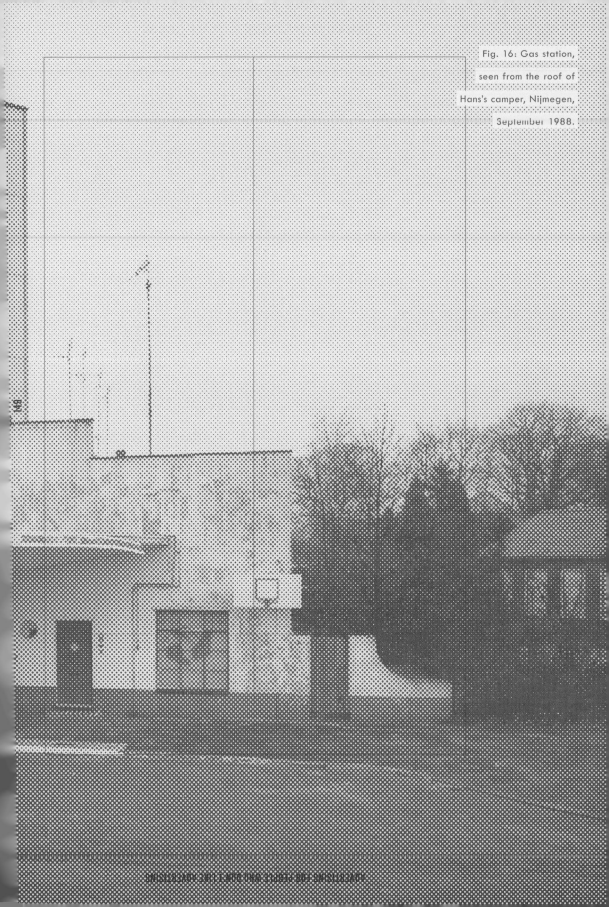

"I took up writing. While on assignment in the municipality of Gent I revisited photography, but it was hopeless. So I stayed in my hotel room and I read the only book I thought was interesting: Sherlock Holmes.

"Here, I got this idea that you can approach photography not for the form but only for the facts that are in the photograph. And that's what I'm doing now: to me a photograph's form is not interesting, but the facts of it are. That was inspired by Sherlock Holmes — just the facts. A photograph is interesting if the facts in the photograph are interesting."

NEWS IS PROBLEMS, ADVERTISING SELLS THE SOLUTIONS.

"You have the feeling that your life is constantly threatened, by evil forces or by your own stupidity, by your mistakes. News shows us these problems and adverts give us possible solutions. In a newspaper you see a dialogue, with the news saying the world's a horrible place, and the adverts saying things will be better 'if you swallow this,' 'if you put this on your face,' 'if you buy this.' So it's like news and ads are two sides of the same whole."

THE BIRTH OF PR.

particularly public relations. He was one of Sigmund Freud's nephews, and he believed in this post-First World War notion that people don't think in a rational way. Instead of tuning into their rational thinking, you should tune into their desires. And that's what you see in communications all the time even today.

"An early example of this from Bernays was when he tried to get women to start smoking. One Easter Day, he hired a little group of suffragettes and told the newspapers that the suffragettes were planning an action. He told the papers when and where they should be in order to witness this event. He didn't explain what exactly would happen. So the papers showed up, and the suffragettes took out cigarettes hidden underneath their skirts. They started smoking. They called it 'The Torch of Freedom.'

"Bernays was a product of the time. After all this production of military goods, America had been turned into a mass-production society. How to get people to buy all this stuff? In this climate, there was suddenly a lot of space for ideas about advertising."

ADVERTISING, AS SEEN BY A JOURNALIST.

"What I like about advertising is how it cleverly combines image and text. In newspapers, image and text are divided. So you have this group of photo editors and this group of guys who write the stories, and they're always separate. In advertising, you have the copywriter and the art director and they team up, and I think that's a very interesting way of producing messages.

"I like advertising because it's much more cleverly made than journalism. Because of this art director/copywriter team, you end up with more possibilities for contradiction between the headline and image, for instance. In the newspaper it's impossible to work that way. As a photo editor, the only feedback you get is: 'the elements in the picture do not fit the text.' And so you have to change the picture.

"Journalism always favours text over images. The picture has to legitimize the text. The exception to this are some of Rupert Murdoch's papers, where the interplay between text and image is much better."

ADVERTISING, MEET JOURNALISM.

"The most straightforward way in which journalism becomes a form of advertising is press releases. Seventy-five percent of what you read is based on a press release. People still don't know that most of what they're reading is a form of advertising.

"There are various reasons for this. One is the cut-backs in journalism. As a journalist you don't have so much time any more. There are far fewer journalists at their desks, so you are forced to cut corners and use all this free publicity stuff to fill space.

"Another factor is that the line between a press release and news is often vague, even to a journalist. This is because press releases are frequently offered through the news agencies. In this way, an extra layer is added. The journalist thinks, 'Oh, this is from the news agency, it must be legitimate,' but the news agency gets it from the business people.

"So, primarily, it's market forces that have led us here. I think pure journalism is investigation, but this isn't the case any more, albeit with rare exceptions like The Guardian. The noble reasons for getting into journalism, finding the truth and so on, are still used to attract people to the profession, but really it's mostly PR now.

"Here's a fairly extreme illustration of this. If you go to the website of ANP, that's the Dutch news agency, and you want stories for your company or your sports club or your group, you just pay for it. Buy a headline. If it's really interesting and everybody reads your story, then you don't even have to pay. So you cut out the middle man: there's no PR agency, there's no advertising agency.

"But there are subtler versions of this process. For instance, if you have a demonstration, and you don't have any press, then there wouldn't be a demonstration. fig. 17 The demonstration happens because the organizers know the press is going to be there."

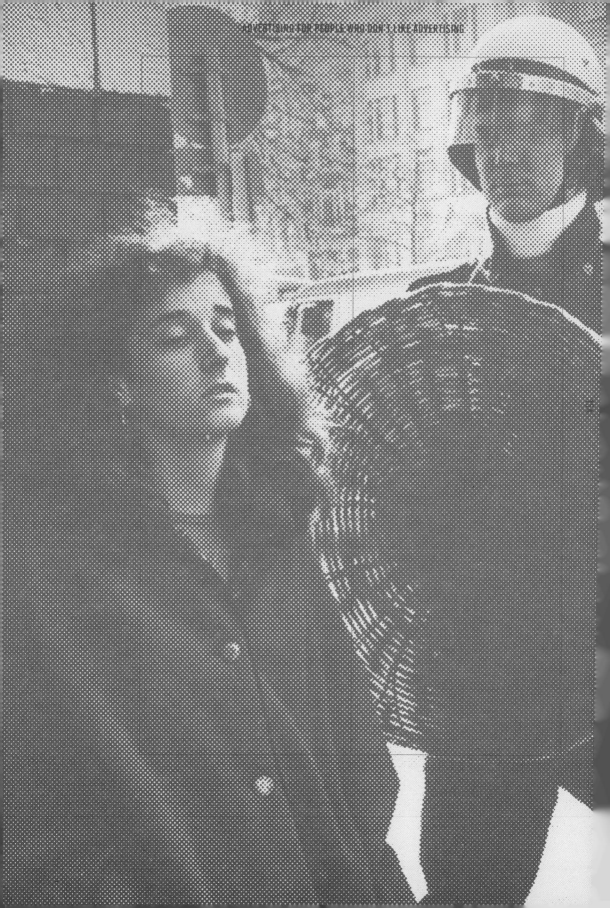

Fig. 17:
A typical image of conflict as
represented in newspapers. Taken
during the crowning of Holland's
Queen Beatrix, April 1980.

THE UNEXPECTEDLY HONEST BUSINESS OF ADVERTISING.

"I think journalism is more unethical than pure advertising. I think advertising is honest about what it wants. Journalism on the other hand is hidden, but it's still mostly advertising.

"Having said that, I don't like to think in moral terms about things because it makes it harder to see the possibilities and to discover things. When I grew tired of the structures in images from photojournalism it was because they were dull and predictable, not because they were morally wrong.

"In my work, I like to get across how rich everything is and discover new possibilities. If you start looking at things in one way, it's just like wearing a certain set of glasses. Every time you change those glasses, everything changes, your whole perspective changes.

This happened every time I changed my style of photography — you start interpreting things in a different way. In the case of advertising, if an ad changes how you view the world, then it's an acceptable form of advertising. VW is an example of a brand that does this consistently. What I like about the old VW ads is that they're treating the public like adults, daring to talk about their product in a negative way.

"When I don't like something in advertising or journalism, it's the clichés I dislike, not the moral issues. That's what I step back from."

ON THE OTHER HAND.

"However, what I do think is that it would probably be better for society if people wouldn't be so happy with owning stuff, with materialism. If you are more interested in things in the world around you, then you are no longer interested in actions that make other people unhappy.

"And what advertising teaches you is how to get ideas across, so maybe you can use that skill for something else, for getting desires to go in a direction that has nothing to do with materialism."

UNDERESTIMATING THE MEDIA.

"If you take the widest perspective, I think the news is really, really very important in how we perceive the world. Much more so than pure advertising, which ultimately is only about selling stuff."

"Nevertheless, often advertising techniques are used by people trying to get in the news. An example of this is the Tea Party. They're being focused on the whole time. If the Tea Party does something, you see all these pictures at the press agencies. Why? Well, Rupert Murdoch's people helped them, gave them courses. For instance, the Tea Party used to print their demonstration boards. However, they stopped after they were advised that handmade boards would be seen as more genuine, as a really personal expression of feeling. That's a kind of advertising. It's corporate."

DO YOU THINK JOURNALISM IS BECOMING LESS LIKE ADVERTISING BECAUSE OF SOCIAL MEDIA?

MAKE NEWS NEW.

"In order to make advertising that I'd like, you first need a new concept of news. I think it's connected. News and advertising: it's all media. But what that new form of advertising/news would be, I don't know.

"But I'd like to experiment in this area, maybe through a little magazine, and try to find new ways of finding interesting things to tell other people. It would be all about avoiding clichés, and treating people like grown ups."

"In some ways, journalism is going back to its pure investigative roots because regular people are handling the entertainment side of the news online, via blogs and Twitter. Fast facts and PR-style stories, that's increasingly covered by Twitter. What's really behind the facts, that will become journalism again."

MARK FENSKE ON TEACHING

ADVERTIS-ING LIKE ARISTOTLE

Mark Fenske has been a creative at Young & Rubicam, and at Wieden + Kennedy, Portland. He started his own music video production/ ad agency hybrid called The Bomb Factory in L.A. There, he directed music videos for Van Halen, among others. Mark has won the MTV Video of the Year, Director of the Year, and is a member of the Screen Actors' Guild. He's also received every major advertising prize. Mark now teaches creative thinking at the Virginia Commonwealth University.

PLEASE DESCRIBE YOUR BACKGROUND.

"I am a Midwestern boy.

A Michigan-football-watching, deep-fried-turkey-eating, flannel-shirt-is-a-coat man of the prairie.

A barn-sized door-filler from the offensive tackle-producing breadbasket of the country.

Things unrefined, unrecommended and unbeautiful arouse me, touch me with a

kinsman's embrace, and speak to me in a dialect unhearable to those who could watch the 1985 Chicago Bears' Super Bowl Shuffle and remain tearless.

When I sit down to write, beer and sausage is what flows in my head.

I am uncommonly claustrophobic and I am a sinner in need of salvation.

In short, just like everyone else, maybe shy a couple of style points."

GIVEN THAT THIS BOOK IS CALLED "ADVERTISING FOR PEOPLE WHO DON'T LIKE ADVERTISING," WE'RE OBLIGED TO ASK: DO YOU LIKE ADVERTISING?

"Nobody asks astronauts if they like space. Or priests if they like God. But everyone asks advertising folks if we like advertising.

They say it the way you might ask a stripper if he or she likes stripping.

I like advertising. I'd rather be in advertising than be an astronaut.

Mostly because I saw The Right Stuff and am pretty sure I don't have it.

But also because everything astronauts

do stays in their head.

They see the Earth from space.

Which is cool.

But what do they do with that experience?

Now, if I could be an astronaut
who gets a job as a copywriter after
being on the moon.

That'd be some sweet action.

Ninety-eight percent of the advertising
people see is crap.

No wonder they wonder why we like it.
If they knew what the other 2% is like,
and the power of it, and what it's like to
make it up out of nowhere, they'd like it
like I do."

WHAT ARE THE BITS YOU DON'T LIKE?

"Everything in life is both good and bad.

Awards, for example, often go to look-
alike work rather than to ground-breaking
leaps forward.

Which is bad.

But what does a better job than the
awards shows of keeping track of who
did what when?

Good and bad in everything.

At the present time something to hate
about advertising is the deleterious effect
on the quality of the work that the holding
companies are having."

HOW WOULD YOU CHANGE THOSE BITS FOR THE BETTER?

"Teach what good work is, show folks how to do it, and not ever accept anything less than good work from them and they will grow up to want good work.

You can't argue with a holding company. You have to beat them."

HOW WOULD YOU DEFINE A "GOOD IDEA"?

"I'm glad you asked this question because it gives me a chance to point at Milton Glaser.

I've never read a better explanation than that on page 7 of his book, Art is Work:
1. Work that goes beyond its functional intention and moves us in deep and mysterious ways we call great work.
2. Work that is conceived and executed with elegance and rigor we call good work.
3. Work that meets its intended need honestly and without pretense we call simply work.
4. Everything else, the sad and shoddy stuff of daily life, can come under the heading of bad work."

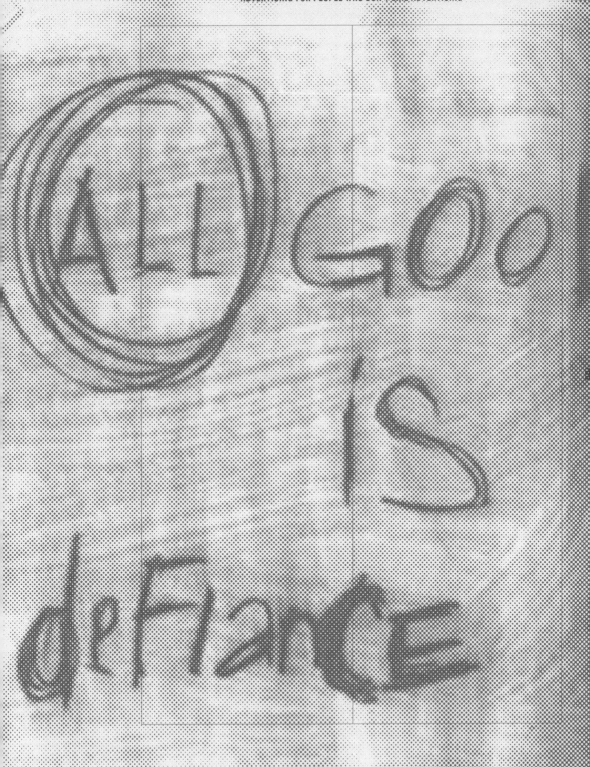

done in

MANAGEMENT.

A sketch from Fenske's workbook, created during his time in L.A., where he ran production company/ ad agency The Bomb Factory.

MORE GENERALLY, HOW WOULD YOU DEFINE CREATIVITY?

"I don't think any of the general definitions help.

Making stuff up?

Of course.

But what's interesting is to consider there's nothing we can make up that didn't exist to begin with.

Nothing that wasn't made up before we got to it."

WHAT EXAMPLES OF CREATIVE WORK REALLY STAND OUT?

"Buckminster Fuller's geodesic dome.

Michelangelo's David.

Oh, you mean ads.

I thought the Grrr spot for Honda in London was great.

And 1984.

They're the equal of anything else on Earth.

But, at the same time, they're not Bach, they're not Twain, they're not Rembrandt. Ads, as part of their format and intention, tie themselves to the ground.

Literature and music and painting fly."

WHO ARE YOUR HEROES? (CAN BE AD PEOPLE OR PEOPLE IN GENERAL.)

"Abraham Lincoln, Martin Luther King, Walt Disney, Sandy Koufax, Emily Dickinson is a start. Ad guys: Hal Riney."

WHAT ARE THE ATTITUDES THAT CREATIVES NEED TO SURVIVE?

"Selfishness.

Also, you can't be afraid of being naïve. Because you can only find satisfaction in satisfying what your naïve heart wants."

HOW WOULD YOU RATE THE QUALITY OF YOUNG CREATIVES LEAVING COLLEGE TODAY?

HERE'S AN OLDIE: DO YOU BELIEVE CREATIVITY IS INNATE AND CAN BE DEVELOPED?

"They don't read much, so I'm not sure where they've gotten it all from, but they're smarter than I remember myself being at their age.

As ad folks, though, they're more inclined toward measuring success according to the business side of things than I was, and more than I admire.

Maybe that's their intelligence kicking in. I think advertising (the 2% that's made right, at least) is the most powerful art form on Earth.

I fear the next group doesn't see it that way and, as a result, may not value it enough to keep it powerful."

"I don't know.

I do wonder, though.

I wonder if creativity might be like kissing. You're born with an ability to pucker your lips and press them against another person's.

You can add to your ability by practising. And you might develop a repertoire of tricks if you have experience with other kissers.

But.

What if you're a genius kisser right out of the box? Then aren't all the tricks

you've added a perversion of
your genius?

That's only a rare problem.

But it is one, so it bears mentioning.
The more common problem is that kissers
tend to make other kissers kiss like they do.
So what we think are new tricks and
clever moves are in practice actually a
kind of corralling of our natural free-form
instincts that keeps us closer to the habits
of the pack and steers us away from
genuine invention.

Then there's the matter of what
constitutes joy.

Is it greater to kiss a tutored mouth or
one lacking artifice?

I don't see how it's possible that
every human being isn't born with
the creative impulse.

This is because I believe God created
the world and made man to be like him.
So us all having creativity is a given.
When you ask whether it can be

developed I think the answer is
equally obvious.

Of course it can.

But, like kissing, it needs to be done
by the person who owns it. In search
of what he or she naïvely wants."

Failure is g
Big failure
Big, ignom
failure in fi
lot of peop
best.

ood.

s better.

nious

ont of a

e is the

WHAT'S YOUR PERSONAL APPROACH TO TEACHING COMMERCIAL CREATIVITY?

"Yes, that's the exact right practical question to follow the abstract philosophical question before it.

I believe we learn by doing.

Aristotle said this a long time ago and I'm proud to say I agree with him.

It is especially true in making art. Now, a person can argue whether advertising is art.

But to me that argument doesn't matter here because, whether you consider the end product to be art or not, the person making it up has to approach it as an art form.

The impulse that starts a sculpture or a painting or a bridge or a song is there in the making of an ad because, like those other art forms, an ad is a thing constructed out of other things.

That one of the considerations which influences the shape of an ad is a concern for how it makes the audience feel about bathroom tile cleaner doesn't mean the maker of the ad is released from the other obligations of an art form, such as it having to entertain, be beautiful, release joy in the viewer and whatever else art does.

So, to get better at an art form, how does one proceed?

Do it.

Do it without regard for what has been done before.

Do it by your own lights and what God has given you to bring you to the point you're at.

Then.

When you've made something, stand there while other people look at it.

Drink in their disapproval.

Savour their jealousy when you do something right.

Feel.

That builds steel in your gut.

It might be steel that tells you don't do _____ again.

Or it might be steel that tells you to, yes, walk down that dark hallway leading nowhere in your mind because last time you did so you found what other people wished they'd found.

That steel comes from you putting your work in front of people and eating the results.

Then.

I'm not saying there's no room for a teacher.

There are formats to be learned for each different art form — how to handle marble if you're a sculptor, what a script should look like on a page if you want actors to be able to read their parts, or why you might consider making a sentence sound one way as opposed to another in order to have it fit into a newspaper ad.

These format questions require a teacher.

Plus.

What I think is the real contribution a teacher makes:
Putting a high standard in front of the student.

And then holding them to it.

Perhaps my constructing that line in two partial sentences gives some indication as to which of the two is the harder to do."

Do it again and do it again.

WHAT LESSONS HAVE YOU PERSONALLY LEARNED OVER YOUR YEARS IN ADVERTISING? WHICH APHORISMS HELP YOU GET THROUGH A HARD DAY?

"The best help I've gotten in becoming better at advertising, and have passed on to others, is found in the writing of Ralph Waldo Emerson.

Specifically in his essay 'Self Reliance,' Emerson, speaking against the tendency we all have to not trust our own thoughts, exhorts each person to be who they are, think what they think and stand on what occurs to them as soon as they think it. And to especially do so when the tide of public opinion is most against them. Following this advice may never make sense to you in the short-term, but not following it will make you quite unhappy with yourself in the long-term."

HOW WOULD YOU SAY THAT EDUCATION AFFECTS STANDARDS OF CREATIVITY IN OUR SOCIETY GENERALLY?	"The more smart, funny, beautiful, truthful ads we make the smarter, funnier, more beautiful and truthful the world becomes. Do schools help this happen?
	No. Schools are organizations built upon money.
PUT ANOTHER WAY: YOU COULD ARGUE THAT EVERY	People make education happen.
JOB POTENTIALLY INVOLVES A	A school does not have standards of excellence.
DEGREE OF CREATIVE THINKING.	People do.
WOULD YOU SAY WE ENCOURAGE THAT ASPECT IN HOW WE TRAIN YOUNG PEOPLE AT SCHOOLS AND UNIVERSITIES?	It has always been so."

WHERE DID ALL THE REBELS?

GO? INTERVIEW

WITH STEVE HENRY.

Steve Henry was creative director and co-founder of HHCL, an agency renowned for breaking the many rules and assumptions in advertising. *Campaign* magazine voted it Agency Of The Decade, and Henry was named one of the forty most influential British advertising people in the last fifty years. Here, he talks about HHCL, the current state of advertising and where he sees communications heading.

BEING GOOD MEANS BEING AMBIVALENT.

"I think the best people in our industry are very ambivalent about it. They like it and they hate it at the same time.

"What interests me about advertising is the interception between commerce and creativity, and I think that's what keeps a lot of very bright people in

the industry, despite all the frustrations and all the drawbacks.

"The opportunity to use your creativity with such a fine commercial ambition is utterly fascinating. Otherwise the commercial world is pretty much bereft of creativity.

"About twelve years ago I was emailing for a while with Jelly Helm, a copywriter at Wieden + Kennedy for a long time. We were emailing each other because we both had an interest in green issues; this was back in 2001 or 2002. Jelly started seeing the immorality in advertising and said he couldn't work in it anymore.

"His point was that if the rest of the world consumes at the rate America consumes, we would need four more planets to provide the raw materials. What that exposes is that the levels of consumption in Western society are not sustainable and not healthy. Advertising essentially encourages this consumption and desire.

"Once Jelly got that thought in his head, he couldn't work in advertising any more. Once I got that thought in my head,

I struggled. And I think a lot of people struggle to work in advertising if they know that concept.

"After all, what we want to do is increase the market. But if consumption is already excessive, what are we doing?

"At HHCL we were concerned with this, and we came up with this phrase: 'responsible demand.' But we couldn't get traction with clients on it: they didn't want to hear it. And you can understand why. It's enough being a client in an incredibly competitive marketplace, never mind having your advertising agencies talk about the morals of what you're doing.

"When I do talks, I do raise this question and leave it with the audience by saying: 'What do we do about this?' And so far I haven't got a good answer back."

ARE AD PEOPLE CONCERNED BY ADVERTISING'S LESS ADMIRABLE ASPECTS?

"I think they push them aside. I think the advertising industry is full of bright and nice people, but not as many radicals as I'd like. And not enough people who are genuinely troubled by it.

"Over the last few years I think society started getting better. Acceptance of climate change, recycling and a feeling of increased responsibility. I think society in general has moved in the right direction. Advertising has ended up with a bit of that, but I don't think the industry as a whole has become more responsible.

"The credit crunch hit advertising badly. Advertising had been cut back to the bone, even before the crunch happened. There was no fat anywhere, and agencies were very lean. Clients got more and more demanding, they wanted more for less. Also, the industry is being run by people who understand the bottom line, but not creativity. Advertising used to be about making interesting stuff, now it's about making money.

"The only interesting agencies are private ones. Mother is still interesting because Robert Saville keeps it private. If he sold it, that would be the kiss of death. I work at an agency called Albion, in Shoreditch, that I love. Partly because the partners are very bright, and partly because it's private.

"In the UK, unfortunately, there's a prevalent business model where agencies aim to sell within three to five years. That's all about money and that doesn't make the industry more responsible. Quite the opposite."

ADVERTISING UNDERCOVER.

"There's another issue. We're moving into a situation in which advertising has a very different relationship with culture and content. We're creating content, which I think is a very good thing for creativity within the industry. But that raises massive moral issues. Such as: where are the boundaries between editorial and advertising?

"Also, product placement is now being allowed in British TV programmes. Now, I'm a huge fan of that from a creative point of view. I want to be able to create culture for clients. But morally it makes advertising much more dubious, because you don't know whether you're being sold to or simply entertained.

"A few years ago in America there was a debate about buzz agents. These were people joining discussions online — paid to do so in order to push a particular company's products. In an online discussion you don't know whether people are genuinely offering their opinions or whether they're being paid to offer their opinions."

HHCL.

"I'd worked at two hot shops: GGT and WCRS. We started HHCL in 1987 and the key driving force was a guy called Adam Lury, who is the L of HHCL. He didn't like advertising at all, and was very suspicious about it. He was very left wing, a great feminist and a great radical, about the most radical thinker I've ever come across in the industry. His attitude, which I loved, was: let's just break the rules wherever we can.

"We put reception in the middle of the agency, so visitors found themselves amongst people working, and had to search for reception. We brought tissue meetings over from the States, where you stuck every reference and half-thought idea on a wall, and worked through them with the client. We had open-plan offices, no departments sitting together. We challenged the income structure of advertising: we moved to a fee-based structure. We challenged BARB, which was the body measuring TV ratings. We did that with a full-page ad in The Sunday Times, which ended up losing us one of our clients.

"We invented media strategy. The whole idea was really to shake things up. The best compliment I would get was people coming up to me and saying: 'I saw this weird thing on TV last night. It had to come from HHCL.'

"HHCL had a particular structure for approaching a commercial problem. I still think it's the best way. We would sit down and we'd look at the client's sector, and we'd try and figure out what the underlying, unconscious rules were governing that marketplace. Every market has them. They exist because, somewhere along the line, someone's done something that was perceived to have been a success, and when that happens everybody else follows their rules.

"Our process was very methodical: let's find those rules. That might include how the product is portrayed, or how the consumer is portrayed. And we would map those out, we would tell the clients what those rules were. We would then

show the client work that systematically broke different rules and we'd say: 'You're going to feel uncomfortable about this, but there's no point in doing stuff that doesn't break the rules because the resulting work will be invisible.'

"That's the thing I have a real horror for in this industry. Ninety-eight percent of it just is invisible. It's just money pissed down the gutter. Actually, the industry is a criminal waste of money.

Someone told me that the return on investment for a conventional advertisement in the UK is 56p in a pound. So that means for every pound that the client spends they only get 56 pence back. That's worse than the banking industry. It's a fucking scandal. And it's because people don't have the balls to take risks. If they took risks, then advertising would work.

"We have to do a good job for our client. But if we want to do that, we have to break the rules, which is what interests me. That's what HHCL was about. It was about a place that just loved breaking

rules with intelligence. That's why we were successful for probably fifteen or sixteen years.

"We had a phrase, 'professional radicals,' which probably summed up HHCL's thinking. That description came along seven years into the company. It wasn't a bad description."

HOW TO SELL CHALLENGING WORK.

"Selling work like Tango is hard, but at the same time this is an industry based on niches. The biggest ad agencies only ever have 4% of the market, so you don't need to appeal to all clients everywhere. You only need to appeal to a minority to sustain a working business. At any one point, there are going to be only between 10% and 20% of clients interested in doing stand-out work. Once we'd defined where we were coming from, it worked very well.

"What happened was: the intermediaries would put together pitches for the client and say, 'What do you want then?' And the client would say: 'We need a network, we need this or that.' Then the intermediaries would say: 'Why don't you talk to HHCL as well, because you don't know what they are going to come back with.'

"That was great. We were up against multinational networks. We hadn't qualified to win the business but people wanted to see what we were going to bring to the party. Nothing is easy in advertising, but, still, it was relatively okay for a time because we had a reputation for doing something that we enjoyed, and a significant number of clients were interested in exploring with us."

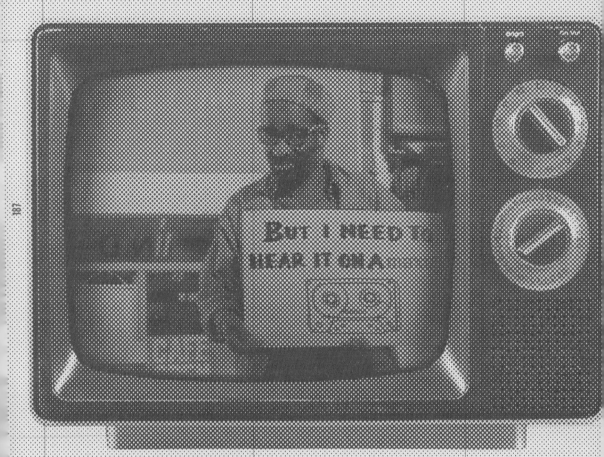

187

Fig. 19: A scene from HHCL's ground-breaking (and sometimes controversial) Tango ads.

WHICH JOBS GAVE HHCL CREATIVE FREEDOM?

"There were three or four projects at various stages. We did some work for Maxell tapes that won the Grand Prix at Cannes ^{fig. 18} — even though we didn't even enter it because we didn't believe in awards systems. The production company entered it instead.

"We'd always, just always wanted to be outlaws. That's what interested us. But then we did Maxell and people went: 'Oh hang on, these guys can do stuff that wins major awards.'

"Then I think Tango was not just award-winning but phenomenally successful. Working with the client was just a dream. He wanted bold, groundbreaking work. It was a joy. ^{fig. 19}

"And then the launch of First Direct was my favourite campaign we ever did. That was completely and utterly radical in every respect. That was a phenomenally successful brand launch.

"We rebranded the AA as 'The Fourth Emergency Service,' which Campaign magazine called 'the smartest bit of thinking that ever came out of an ad agency.' I don't think it is, but I happily quote it because it's a nice thing to have said about you.

"So, we were doing radical work. But I think when we did Tango, First Direct and the AA people said: 'Hang on, this radical stuff achieves commercial success.' First Direct is still the only brand that exists in the financial marketplace. There's no other bank that is a brand, and we did that twenty years ago. It was a phone bank when we launched it. It had no high-street profile to it, but it became a very successful bank.

"The AA went from 8 million to 11 million subscribers on the back of our rebrand. Tango went from selling 1 million cans a day to 1.3 million cans a day, because we did some outstanding advertising for them."

THE INTERNET ON TV.

"A lot of our work was TV-based but worked more like Internet advertising today. It involved people. That was right at the heart of it, and it was a very Adam Lury thing. Adam really got that brand building meant making communities for clients. People felt more part of that community because it was interactive. We asked people to switch channels during ads. We loved to turn the volume up and down, or we asked people to video our commercials. We put phone lines on the end of our Tango ads. We sold products for Tango. It was all about trying to generate communities around a sense of bold work, work that stood for something.

"Our brands were about making the world a better place, one in which brands were on the side of consumers, where we broke rules and engaged people. That was it in a nutshell."

AFTER HHCL.

"Mother's creative director Robert Saville once gave us a big compliment, saying that the people at Mother were only in advertising because of HHCL. I think at one point we were a beacon for mavericks. People realized: 'Oh hang on, you can actually have fun and break the rules.'

"But we sold out, which was our big mistake. It was doomed after that.

"The climate of advertising now is really unhealthy, but the future of advertising is interesting.

"I'm involved in various product and brand launches at the moment. I don't want to use conventional advertising, I don't want to use conventional ad agencies.

"The model that I think works best is an online community site like Netmums. The founder is Siobhan Freegard, who launched Netmums because after she had

a baby she felt lonely and she wanted to connect with other mums. She began it without any commercial ambition at all. Today, she's got a million mums online around the country.

"Any brand manager will tell you that mums are the key decision-makers in virtually every commercial household judgment, from the holiday to the car to getting a new house. Mums make the decisions. They are incredibly powerful and ridiculously overlooked by the male-dominated ad industry.

"Siobhan was telling me about three projects she had done with clients. One was the Sainsbury's marketing department, which wanted more people to go online. Another was a brand manager for a soft drink company — the drink had been criticized for its content, was it healthy for kids or not? Then there was someone who wanted to launch a green washing powder.

"So all of those product launches had to do with negative perceptions and the clients wanted to change consumer behaviour. Those are exactly the problems that ad agencies are supposed to solve. In all three of those cases, the clients just talked to Siobhan instead. She took them online to discuss these topics, and consumers shared their problems. Together, you co-create an answer to the problem.

"The Sainsbury's marketing director ended up with a lot of people who were willing to try online shopping, which was exactly what he wanted. He was able to incentivize them in the right way, so he wins.

"The soft drinks guy was able to change perceptions about his drink by explaining exactly what the contents of his drink were, and how they weren't unhealthy.

"And the guy launching the green washing powder was able to launch his product with consumers, to try it with them. They tried it, they fed back.

"The cost in all three cases was practically nothing. Siobhan wanted to get involved because these are interesting topics for her mums. The mums who liked these projects

self-selected and came aboard. They became advocates and co-creators of that brand, and it's all free.

"It's also how Albion launched Giffgaff, which is a new phone carrier from O2. Here again, it's all about subscribers helping each other. Not relying on a parent organization, but a peer-to-peer support system. Building a community. And that's the future.

"But you've got to do it with integrity, and you've got to do it in a way that interests people.

"What we're discussing screws the old advertising model. It doesn't fit. If I'm being optimistic, I still think that there will be a role for advertising agencies. I'm hoping that the industry will see that what they really need is brave creative thinking.

"At the minute, this isn't happening. The industry is just full of people who service clients, who are desperate to hang on to clients for the income that they give. They don't challenge clients and they produce

crap. Alex Bogusky said this: 'It has become a service industry.'

"We need to be a product industry. We need to be an industry that actually makes interesting stuff for our clients. Advertising needs to get its confidence back and say: 'We can do this.' We have to make work that enters culture, that tells you a story in an interesting way. I think the industry desperately needs to get back to cherishing and celebrating creativity."

TEACH
US
REBELLION.

"I have two kids, twenty-one and eighteen. The twenty-one-year-old is studying to be a vet, and the eighteen-year-old has been offered a place at Oxford. So they're both very bright.

"But that generation has been tested and examined remorselessly since they were tiny kids. I fucking hate it, but it's the system. And they've had to play that system.

"The education development expert Ken Robinson talks a lot about failure, that you have to fail, and that you have to allow and encourage failure. If you talk to the former creatives at HHCL, they'll say that this was the greatest freedom I gave them, this sense that they could experiment and even fail.

"We're stuck in a culture that worships money and worships success, in a really dangerously narrow way. I just hope there's a backlash. Once something has been in place for a while, the next generation will rebel against it, will go: 'Fuck that!'

"I hope we will see a rebellion against blind consumerism. I hope we will see a rebellion against this remorseless bottom-line success ethic and choose exactly what Ken Robinson mentions: choose exploration, failure and experimentation. That's what being alive is about."

THE LAWS OF CREATIVITY AND

HOW TO MESS WITH THEM.

Many things in life require laws. Life in general requires laws. Laws are what stop us from strolling to the supermarket naked, marrying our pet dogs or invading a neighbouring country on a rampant whim.

But there is one group that staunchly, almost arrogantly, veers away from the reigning-in that laws demand. Not dictators, but rather, those whose work follows "The Creative Process."

There have been many laws and rules written about The Creative Process and how to make better ideas, presumably directed at those who need to structure their disorganized, unravelling thoughts, or to validate their own thinking.

Think of gentlemen like Wallas, Young, Rossman and Wertheimer. Collectively they sound like they run a global advertising agency with offices in 42 countries. Individually, though, these social psychologists, economists and others like them (none calls themselves artists and most, apart from the odd adman,

have their theories grounded in academia) have attempted to qualify creativity by laying out their ideas in the time-honoured tradition of The Bullet-Pointed List.

By and large, the list goes like this: Immerse; Incubate; Illuminate; Verify; Develop. Or in other words, find out what you are doing, go off and do something else for a while, then come back and finish off what you planned to do in the first place.

Once you have learned the laws of The Creative Process, you can ransack your local, friendly airport newsstand to find robust shelving stacked full of books outlining thousands of tips to improve your creativity. These are skilfully written pieces which, if you are a savvy reader, can often be digested simply by reading their back covers.

Every law, tip or piece of advice, however, requires the friction of those who break them, and most within the creative industry will resist

the threatening noose of immovable guidelines. It has long been argued that creativity comes from the subconscious. That the germination of good ideas is something uncontrollable. Like the hiccups.

Having said that, the creative industries are filled with those who may benefit from the odd nugget of advice, especially because creativity has been set free in these times of speedy technological advancements.

Not only set free, but made more honest and real. It is no longer deemed a mystical entity to be creative. It is no longer seen as tricks performed by druids with magic markers. Every one of us out there is creative in our own way, and has a platform to show that creativity, and those not getting paid to be so sometimes outdo those who are.

With that in mind we are going to break the law that says that there

should be no laws to creativity, by
laying out, in paper and ink, fifteen
laws designed to not seem like laws,
but to be workable all the same.
If they don't act as the aids we wish
them to be, please feel free to break
them into small pieces and rearrange
into something that makes sense.
Send them back to us, and we'll
consider using them for the reprint
of this book, should there be one.

Though the following pieces of advice
are set up for those out there in
the advertising and communications
fields, they can be useful for any who
work in related creative industries.
If you work in a nuclear sub, or dig
graves for a living, their effect may
have limited success. But please prove
us wrong.

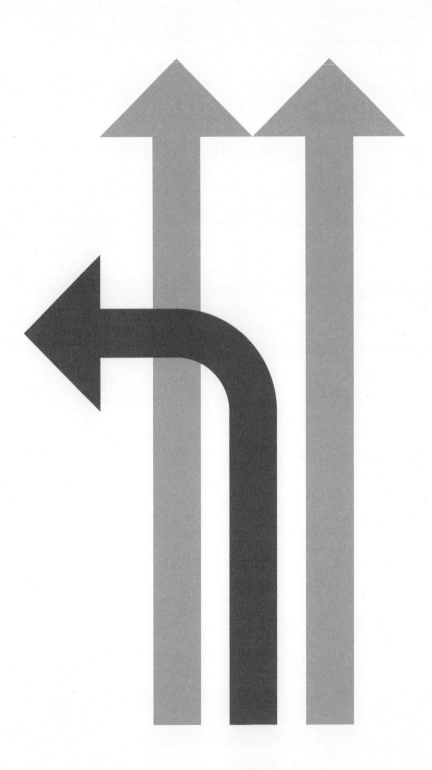

FOLLOW NOT THE PROCESS OF OTHERS.

The teachings of creativity are made to be digested but not regurgitated. Learn, then unlearn. We will all feel comfortable with our own certain fashion of creative process and development — just as some people feel that wearing a beret is so very "now." As examples, we know of those who use a simple digital stopwatch on their laptops to keep themselves in check — the counter makes sure they are working fast and efficiently enough. When they find themselves surfing YouTube for exploding turtles, or going for toilet breaks, they stop the clock and start it when they are actually being properly productive. We know of others out there who spend 99% of their time in graceful, slow-motion dawdling and the remaining 1% engulfed in active and useful creation. There are others that get their creative kicks from being immersed in delirious panic, tearing out clumps of hair with one hand while typing furiously with the other. And those who get buoyed up by the sadistic rantings of anxious creative partners. Whichever process you champion, make sure it's your own. We're all grown ups, we can all be responsible for how we work.

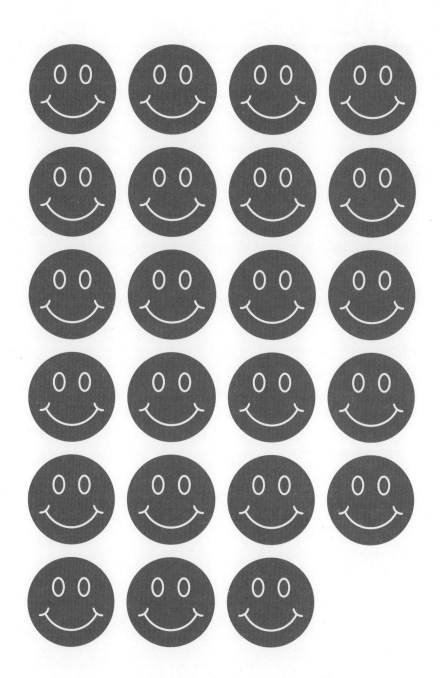

MAKE AND MAKE OFTEN.

There is nothing more debilitating, nothing that paralyzes creativity more than making nothing whatsoever. Cars are fuelled by fossils, Scotland is fuelled by Irn Bru, creatives are fuelled by producing lots of stuff. If you are working somewhere where you haven't made a piece of work in six months, then quit. But make something nice out of your resignation letter, then at least you've made something you're proud of.

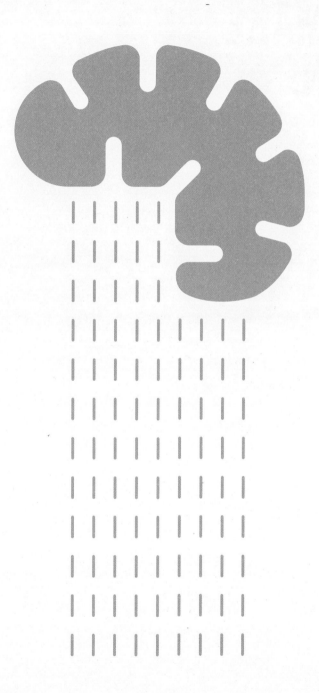

DON'T BRAIN- STORM. NEVER BRAIN- STORM.

Brainstorming is ten people in a room masturbating — slightly embarrassing and always messy at the end. No great problem has ever been solved through brainstorming. Not a single one. Look through the annals of history. There may have been more people in the room/cave. They may even have sat round a table/ rock. However, discussing and scribbling their collective thoughts on a whiteboard did not the eureka moment make. Light drizzles are produced, not storms. Keep the people involved minimal. Fewer brains, more thunder.

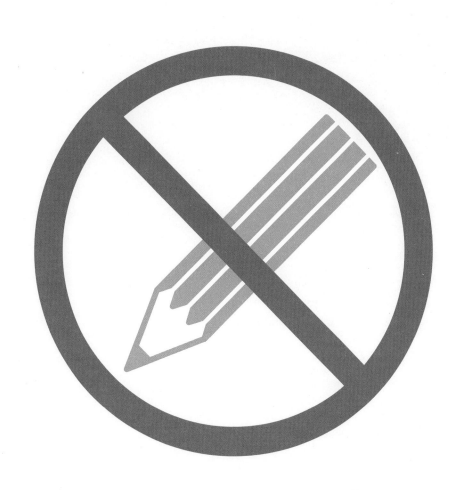

WRITE NOTHING DOWN.

You will go through the first part of your working life writing everything down in a cheap little notebook. You might then go through the next part of your working life writing everything down in an expensive leatherbound notebook. Then you will have learned to write down as little as possible even though, somewhat ironically, your brain cells have depleted considerably. Do yourself a favour. Forgo the notebooks for your own wits. Your brain will filter out all the bad bits.

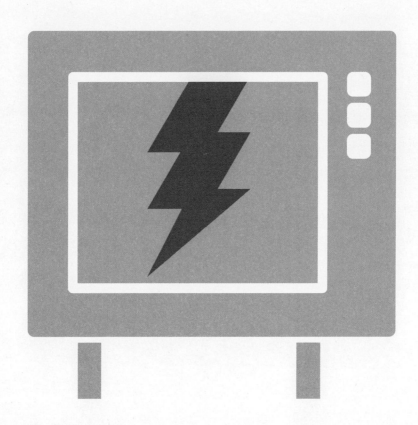

MAKE NEWS NOT ADS.

When people set out to try and make advertising, then that is what they make, with the structure and commonness associated with that. All people avoid advertising, instinctively, even the good stuff. It is better to make news, because people read and are triggered by the news.

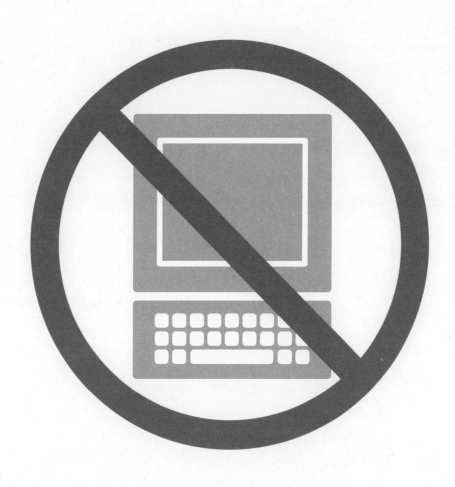

BE LOW-TECH.

Don't get caught up in technology. Sometimes it's a barrier. You end up thinking of where your idea should live, rather than what these ideas should be. Often thinking low-tech is better than thinking hi-tech. Please note, if you are reading this in the future, it still applies.

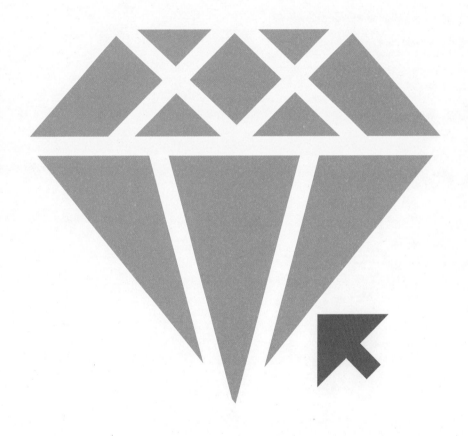

SEIZE UPON FLAWS.

Marketing departments the world over will relentlessly pour upon you the positive benefits of the brand whose problems thine art hath been hired to solve. Smile, clutch the briefing in your hand, shake hands, hug if you will, and walk carefully out of the door closing it silently behind you. Then head to a quiet room and carefully split open the brand until you find its many flaws. Bad often leads to good. Flaws sell as well as advantages. People have flaws, that's why we love them. Brands should do too.

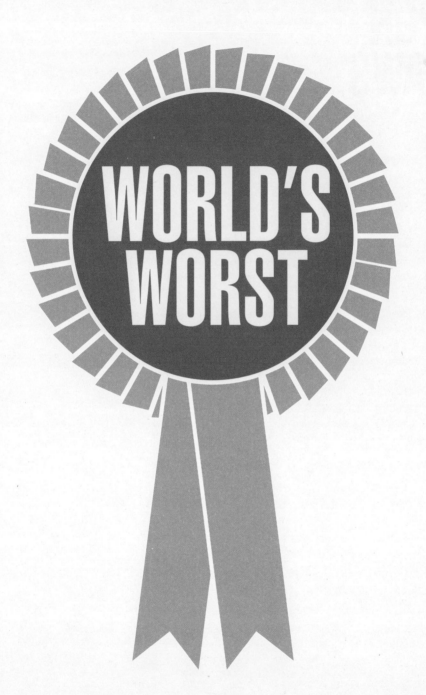

EVERYONE COMPETES TO BE THE BEST. SO BE THE WORST.

The airbrushed best is overrated.
And you are fighting in a crowded
market (everyone wants to be
the best). Proclaim yourself to be
the worst and you will be alone,
and noticed.

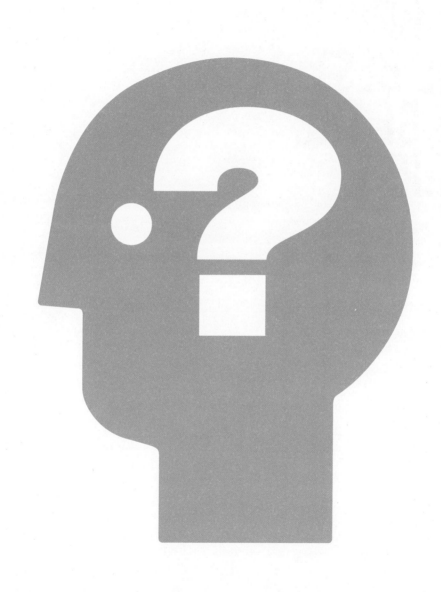

DOUBT IS A SKILL IN SHORT SUPPLY.

There is a section of the advertising and the media industry built on the soft, fleshy foundations of supreme arrogance. You have a skill that they can't quite fathom. You can question your own thoughts, ideas and solutions. That's a good thing, it shows you're human, like the people with whom you are communicating.

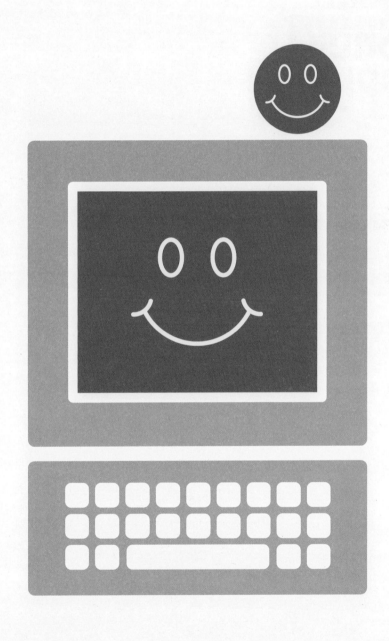

YOUR HOBBY COMES FIRST.

Be you a filmmaker, writer, illustrator or knitting fiend, take your hobby to work with you. You don't work in a bank, your employers shouldn't fire you for using your hobbies to make your work better. Let your hobby fuel your work and vice versa.

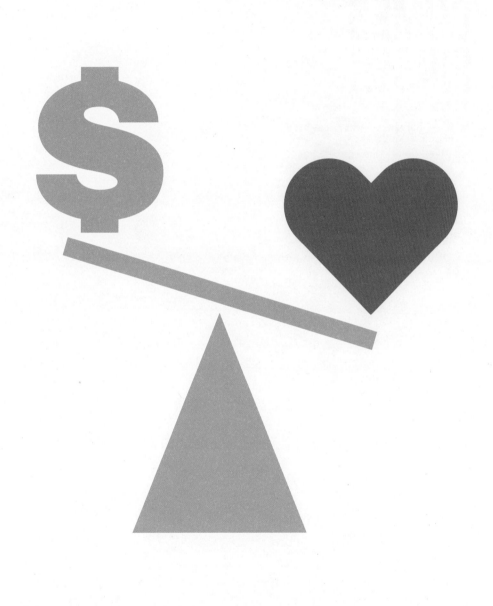

FOLLOW YOUR VALUES RATHER THAN SUCCESS.

We're paraphrasing Einstein here, but we're pretty sure he won't mind. There's not much more to add to this, except that it's not a law, it's a reminder, and it's one that's easy to forget.

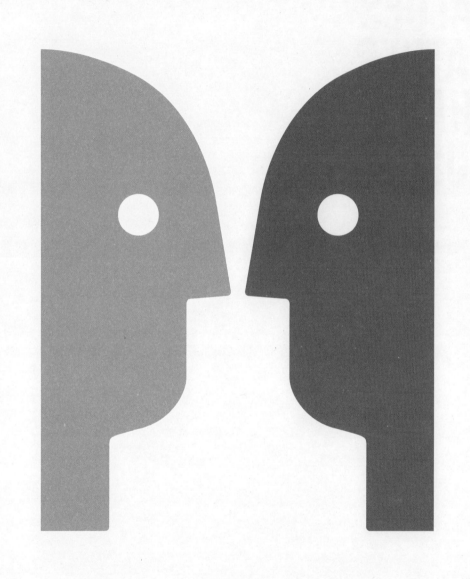

REFLECT REALITY.

Advertising is to communication what plastic surgery is to the healthcare industry. Pointless, vaguely seedy and ultimately producing an overblown, over-saturated version of reality.

If, however, you hold a mirror up to society and show how life really is, rather than indulging in fantasy as the advertising business tends to do, then you are not being dull, you are being switched-on, relevant and ultimately — to use the advertising word du jour — truly "engaging."

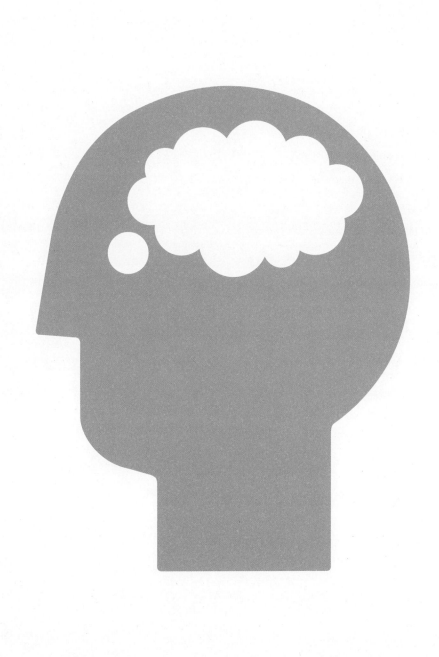

KNOW NOTHING.

Naïvety is a powerful tool. Most people out there pretend to know more than they know. It's better to be honest and listen. And then to know people who know stuff and be a conduit to their knowledge. Beware, however. These people are invariably very dull. Do not invite them around your house, or to be the best man at your wedding.

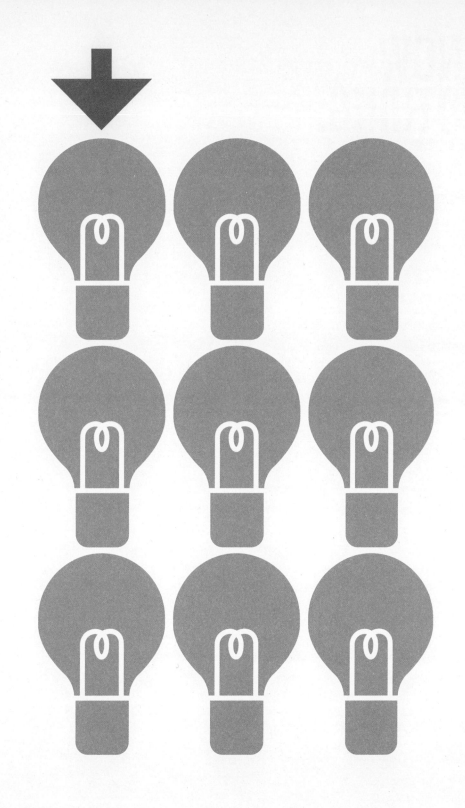

YOUR FIRST INSTINCT WAS RIGHT.

There is a school of thought that
believes that working, reworking
and then reworking again will
produce the best results, while you
punish yourself in the process.
That school of thought is wrong.
First gut instinct tends to beat
your subsequent ideas hands down.
Your instinctual thoughts tend
to be spontaneous, not laboured,
and tend not to be mired in
the many opinions that will invariably
come to cloud your judgement.
Imagine re-cooking a meal over
and over again in a microwave,
then barbecuing it, frying it, boiling
it up and then eating it. Keep it
fresh, it'll taste better.

And if it doesn't, you haven't invested
too much time in it and can always
start over.

THIS FEELS GOOD

MAKE IT MEANINGFUL.

There's a term for this, these days. It's called belief-driven communication. It's about marketing your brand based on social awareness/ social activities and we aren't totally convinced. Is this value-driven side of brands truly meaningful, or a marketing sheen? Being meaningful is more a state of mind than a positioning, and it means showing your social side in all aspects of what you do, from the people you work with to the message you're telling, from the way you portray people in your communication to the recognition that you feel good about what you've done at the end of the day because it has some worth. Being meaningful should come naturally, because creativity and communication are missing a vital ingredient without it.

GOOD

BYE.

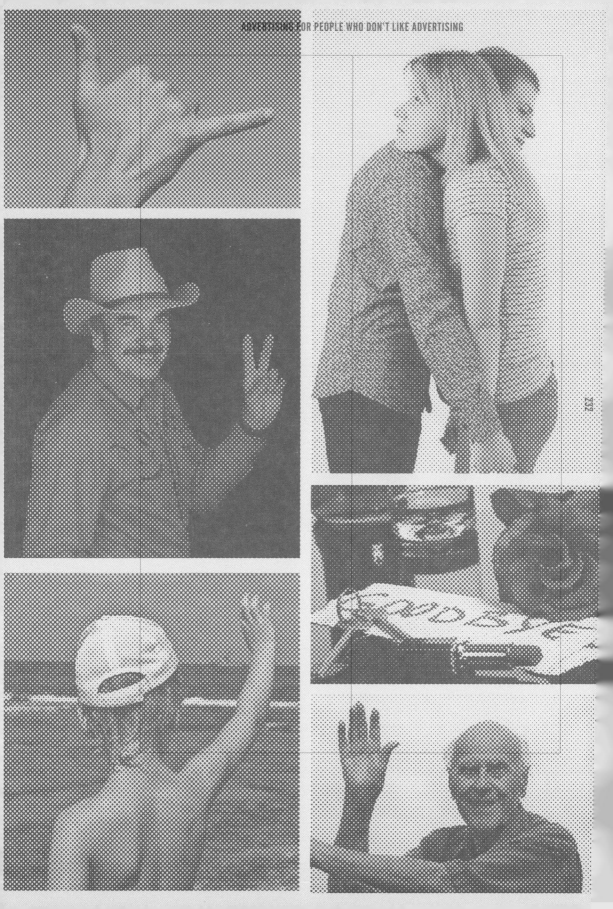

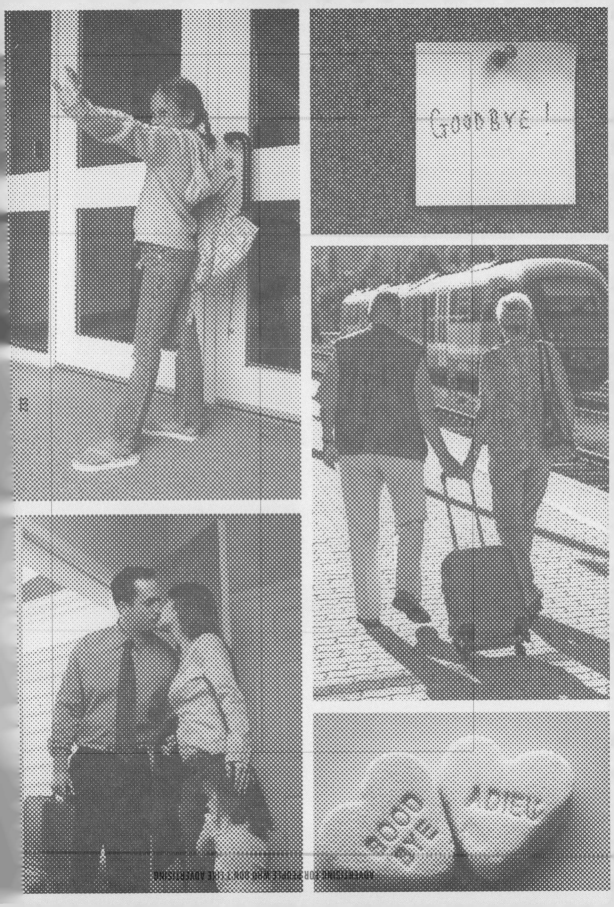

Goodbye !

This is difficult: concluding a book whose purpose was to ask questions, not reach conclusions.

But let's have a go because, as it happens, we've picked up lots to consider.

In these pages, Stefan Sagmeister shared his suggestions for how to make working life less like work and more like life — balanced, saner.

Steve Henry offered a prophecy for advertising that didn't include adverts, but did involve a continual, more egalitarian dialogue between brands and customers.

Hans Aarsman took us on a trip to the misty netherworld where advertising becomes news, and news becomes a series of half-rewritten press releases.

Anthony Burrill spoke his mind through images, while Mark

Fenske explained what it takes to be a stellar young creative.

And Alex Bogusky put forward "Common," a practical, up-and-running alternative to capitalism's systemic problems.

While their opinions are diverse, and while KesselsKramer doesn't always agree, there is a sense of unity. Of course, this comes partly from a straightforward dislike of advertising's current state. But it also stems from a paradox: we have no respect for advertising, but we're all fans.

Not fans in a screaming teenage girl kind of way, idealizing without reflecting. More fans of the weary, middle-aged variety — sticking with a relegated team because we're somehow sure they could be great, despite poor play and bad management.

Re-reading our contributors' words, they're sceptical and occasionally frustrated.

But indifferent?

Nope.

Bored?

Also nope.

And while condemning advertising completely is spectacularly easy, it's much harder to express why, and even more difficult to propose how it can be positively changed. Our interviewees do just that.

In fact, there's advice that — with luck, sweat and optimism — just might work.

Often, very often, there's excitement amongst the criticism, a frequent acknowledgement of advertising's potential, of what it might become, and what it sometimes already is.

It's maybe surprising to hear such passionate views on this stuff, especially if you're

outside advertising, if your
experience of it is being slumped
on the couch watching fake
superheroes unclogging toilets
with miracle cleaner.

But here's the thing:

Combining creativity with commerce
is a kick. Finding ways to help
forward-thinking organizations convey
their message is a unique puzzle,
different from other creative pursuits,
different from any other business.
When it's good, it's awesome:
reaching millions, with the capacity
to move people, make them think,
entertain them.

At the start, we mentioned that
a more accurate name for this
book would have been *Communications
For People Who Don't Like Advertising*.

We could make that more accurate
still: *Communications For People Who
Mostly Dislike Advertising As It Is But
Have A Cautious Appreciation For How
It Could Be.*

Mind you, that wouldn't speak
to so many either.

So that isn't the title.

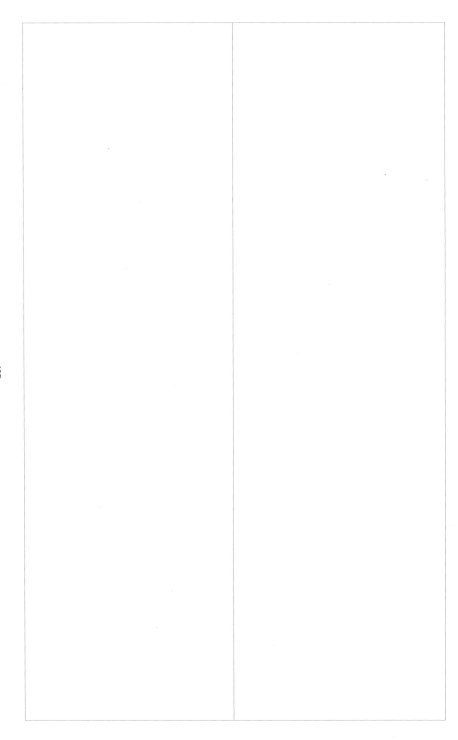

THANKS.

Many, many heartfelt thanks to:
All our contributors, including
interviewees, photographers,
designers, artists, writers and
everyone who works or has
worked with KesselsKramer.

PICTURE
CREDITS.

Cover:
Ox © Ox
P89:
Florent © Teeth ad (1990) by
Dean Lubesky from *Tibor Kalman:*
Perverse Optimist, published
by Booth-Clibborn Editions, 1998
P99:
Sony Bravia © Sony
P102–103:
São Paulo streetview © Stayfly
P110:
Art direction: Stefan Sagmeister;
Production: Bali Rattan, Indonesia;
Photography: Karim Charlebois-
Zariffa; Created: 2009

P112:
"Complaining is silly. Either act
or forget." Art direction: Stefan
Sagmeister; Design: Matthias
Ernstberger, Richard The; Client:
Experimenta Design; Created: 2005
P128–129:
Alex Bogusky, photo ©
m ss ng p eces 2011
P148–149:
Hans Aarsman © Hans Aarsman
P154–155:
Hans Aarsman © Hans Aarsman
P166–167:
Mark Fenske © Mark Fenske
P172–173:
Mark Fenske © Mark Fenske
P187:
Maxell TV © Naresh Ramchandani
and Tim Ashton; Creative Direction ©
Steve Henry and Axel Chaldecott
P188:
Tango Orange © Al Young and
Trevor Robinson; Creative Direction
© Steve Henry and Axel Chaldecott

All other pictures © KesselsKramer

First published in 2012
This paperback edition published in 2013
by Laurence King Publishing Ltd
361–373 City Road
London EC1V 1LR
Tel: +44 20 7841 6900
Fax: +44 20 7841 6910
Email: enquiries@laurenceking.com
www.laurenceking.com

© text and design 2012, 2013 KesselsKramer
This book was produced by Laurence King
Publishing Ltd, London

A catalogue record for this book is
available from the British Library.

ISBN-13: 978 1 78067 320 2

Printed in China

Commissioning editor: Jo Lightfoot
Senior editor: Melissa Danny
Production: Srijana Gurung

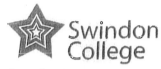